Improving Instruction

Improving Instruction

Best Practices Told through Teacher Stories

J. Casey Hurley

ROWMAN & LITTLEFIELD
Lanham • Boulder • New York • London

Published by Rowman & Littlefield
An imprint of The Rowman & Littlefield Publishing Group, Inc.
4501 Forbes Boulevard, Suite 200, Lanham, Maryland 20706
www.rowman.com

86-90 Paul Street, London EC2A 4NE

Copyright © 2021 by The Rowman & Littlefield Publishing Group, Inc.

All rights reserved. No part of this book may be reproduced in any form or by any electronic or mechanical means, including information storage and retrieval systems, without written permission from the publisher, except by a reviewer who may quote passages in a review.

British Library Cataloguing in Publication Information Available

Library of Congress Cataloging-in-Publication Data

Names: Hurley, J. Casey, 1952- author.
Title: Improving instruction : best practices told through teacher stories / J. Casey Hurley.
Description: Lanham : Rowman & Littlefield, [2021] | Includes bibliographical references. | Summary: "This book provides examples of how K-12 teachers and other instructors improve their instruction"— Provided by publisher.
Identifiers: LCCN 2021025451 (print) | LCCN 2021025452 (ebook) | ISBN 9781475858679 (cloth) | ISBN 9781475858686 (paperback) | ISBN 9781475858693 (ebook)
Subjects: LCSH: Teaching—Methodology. | Teachers—United States—Interviews. | Effective teaching—United States. | Teacher effectiveness—United States.
Classification: LCC LB1025.3 .H87 2021 (print) | LCC LB1025.3 (ebook) | DDC 371.3—dc23
LC record available at https://lccn.loc.gov/2021025451
LC ebook record available at https://lccn.loc.gov/2021025452

This book is dedicated to all the teachers who bring the six virtues of the educated person (understanding, imagination, strong character, courage, humility, and generosity) to their work with young people.

Contents

Acknowledgments — ix
Introduction — xi

PART 1 — 1

1 Stories from Five Elementary School Teachers — 3
2 Stories from Four Middle School Teachers — 17
3 Stories from Eight High School Teachers — 33

PART 2 — 61

4 Stories from a GED Tutor, a Physical Therapist, Two Athletic Coaches, and a Piano Teacher — 63
5 Stories from Two Music Teachers, a Pastor, a Goodwill Trainer, and a Team-Building Consultant — 81

Conclusion — 103
Bibliography — 105
About the Author — 107

Acknowledgments

I appreciate all the people who took the time to tell their stories for this book. Readers will be impressed with their honest revelations about the difficult, creative work they do with young people and other learners.

Introduction

The introduction answers four questions:

1. Why was this book written?
2. How was it written?
3. How are the six virtues of the educated person defined?
4. Where does this book fit alongside other books that tell teachers' stories?

WHY WAS THIS BOOK WRITTEN?

This book was written because, soon after the publication of *The Six Virtues of the Educated Person* (2009), it became apparent that few people want to read philosophy. Instead, people want to read stories. Therefore, this book tells teachers' stories about how they improve their interactions with students to achieve better learning results.

The other reason this book was written is that the argument against the social science paradigm for improving education was made in chapter 8 of *The Six Virtues of the Educated Person* (2009). More than ten years later this paradigm still dominates university teacher and administrator preparation programs. Educators continue to assume that teachers improve instruction by applying the findings of research on effective teaching/administering. Mimicking the medical research model, this improvement paradigm says that teachers depend on education professors. Just as natural scientists conduct experiments to find improved treatments for physical ailments, education researchers conduct social scientific studies to find educational "best practices."

The stories of licensed, public school teachers are in part 1 because all of them have been trained in the social science improvement paradigm. For the past sixty years, university professors have taught aspiring teachers in bachelor's degree programs and experienced teachers in master's degree programs that the way to improve instruction is to apply the findings of research on effective teaching practices. That is why the curricula of these programs routinely cite statistically significant, valid, and reliable results from educational research.

Pioneers in this movement at the University of Wisconsin-Madison in the 1970s and 1980s explained that they were professionalizing teaching and administering by conducting studies that reduced the need for trial and error in schools and classrooms. Educational research methods courses explain that statistically significant findings point to "effective" educational strategies.

This improvement paradigm has found its way into the heart of federal and state education policy. It lives on, today, in programs that promote "evidence-based teaching" and research-based practices.

According to an alumni newsletter from the University of Wisconsin School of Education, researchers from Wisconsin and Minnesota recently won a U.S. Department of Education grant to advance evidence-based practices.

In the press release, the principal investigator said:

> This award brings together a diverse team of experts in areas such as professional learning, evaluation, school leadership, special education, and data analytics to help local, state, and regional educators adopt and refine practices to better serve students.

The press release goes on to say:

> Members of WMCC (Wisconsin-Minnesota Comprehensive Center) have extensive experience working with Wisconsin and Minnesota state education agencies, regional educational support organizations, professional associations, and school districts to translate research into practical applications.
>
> (Kelly, J. L. *Learning Connections*, Winter, 2019–20, p. 21)

The award is for 6.3 million dollars. This project perfectly illustrates the social science improvement paradigm.

The insult and arrogance of this paradigm are astounding, but educators cannot see it because everybody wants instruction to be more "effective." But nobody asks, "effective at what?" The social science improvement paradigm's usual answer is, "effective at teaching students to correctly answer questions on standardized tests." There is nothing wrong with having students get a few more correct answers on standardized tests, but it would be difficult to find a shallower reason for engaging students in school for 6 hours per day, 180 days per year.

During more than twenty semesters of the Foundations of Education course at Western Carolina University, not a single student ever said, "I want to become a teacher to improve students' test scores," even though most of them attended K-12 schools with annual goals focused on improving student test scores. Neither teachers nor students are inspired by the social science improvement paradigm's answer to "effective at what?"

In the Preface to *Teaching as a Performing Art*, Sarason (1999) does not describe the relationship between researchers and practitioners as an insult, but as part of the problem:

> I decided my focus in this book should be on clarifying several things: Why teaching should be taken seriously as a performing art; why teacher preparatory programs are part of the problem and not of the solution. . . . Needless to say this book will be of little or no interest to those who believe that there is little that is basically wrong or self-defeating in the rationale for the selection and training methods of teacher preparatory programs. (p. xi).

Adopting the wrong improvement paradigm means it will take a long time to shift paradigms—to set aside the assumptions underlying it, to pose the questions that lead to meaningful improvement, and to challenge the knowledge that supports it. That is why this book was written—to illustrate the aesthetic paradigm teachers use to improve instruction.

Teachers are artists who improve their performing art (Sarason, 1999) as they:

1. deepen their *understanding* of their subject matter and students,
2. *imagine* how their methods can improve,
3. possess the *strength of character* needed to seek improvement,
4. have the *courage* to try new methods (not knowing their impact),
5. have a *humble spirit* that drives improvement efforts, and
6. have a *generous spirit* that gives time and effort to the needs of their students.

This is an "aesthetic" improvement paradigm because bringing the six virtues to the situation makes learning beautiful, just as bringing the six vices make learning ugly. The educated human nature appreciates deep understanding, creative imagination, strong character, courage, humility, and generosity. The uneducated human nature—which is fraught with ignorance, intellectual incompetence, weak character, fear of truth, pride, or selfishness—makes situations ugly.

The stories in the following chapters told by teachers illustrate that, when teaching is regarded as an art, the path to instructional improvement is clear. It is not clouded by social scientific studies conducted by professors who have never been in the teacher's classroom.

HOW WAS THIS BOOK WRITTEN?

In early spring 2020, administrators in four school districts were asked to nominate elementary, middle, and high school teachers to tell instructional improvement stories. It was explained that this project was not an educational research study but more like a series of newspaper articles on creative teachers. The main difference between these stories and newspaper articles was that teachers had final approval over what was published.

Administrators were asked to think about who they would nominate to attend a conference for creative teachers. Could they think of two elementary, two middle, and two high school teachers? Who would those teachers be?

After administrators recommended teachers in their districts, thirty-minute interviews were scheduled. Meetings took place in classrooms before the pandemic closed schools in late March 2020. Afterward, interviews were conducted on Zoom.

Teachers in part 1 of this book were asked to respond to one of two questions:

1. Do you have a story about how you created one of the best units in your bag of tricks?
2. What do you do to reach your most reluctant learners?

The first step in each session was to decide which story the teacher would tell. Many wanted to tell about how they reached their most reluctant learners because that is a major challenge facing K-12 teachers. All interviews were tape-recorded and transcribed word for word.

In fall 2020, administrators turned down interview requests, saying teachers already had too many additional duties with both online and in-person teaching. After getting several rejections of this type, the project was expanded to include non-school instructors. The result is that part 1 tells improvement stories from seventeen K-12 teachers. Part 2 tells improvement stories from ten non-school instructors.

Stories in part 1 are ordered according to the level of schooling. First, five elementary school teachers tell their stories. Second, four middle school teachers tell their stories. And third, eight high school teachers tell their stories. To maintain anonymity, teachers are identified only by their level of teaching and the order of their story within that level. For example, the first story is from an elementary school teacher (EST1); the last story is from a high school teacher (HST8).

Part 2 tells stories from ten non-school instructors in this order: (1) a GED tutor, (2) a physical therapist, (3) a batting coach, (4) a golf instructor, (5) a piano teacher, (6) a cello instructor, (7) a strings and band teacher, (8) a Baptist pastor, (9) a Goodwill trainer, and (10) an HR consultant specializing in team building. The skills and habits they teach are intellectual, physical, emotional, and spiritual. Their stories responded to the following questions:

1. How has your instruction evolved?
2. What do you do to better connect with your students/clients/parishioners?
3. What do you do to make your instruction clear and simple?
4. What do you do to make sure your instruction is based on proper principles?

Part 1 stories describe teachers instructing young people in school settings, and part 2 stories describe instructors working with students of different ages in different environments.

HOW ARE THE SIX VIRTUES DEFINED?

The six virtues of the educated person were never mentioned to any of the instructors. And none of them could list the virtues if they were asked. Teachers don't describe their work in virtue terms because they don't know the six virtues of the educated person.

The following virtue definitions are adapted from chapter 3 of *The Six Virtues of the Educated Person* (2009). These definitions are the framework for analyzing the stories in parts 1 and 2.

Two Intellectual Virtues

The human mind works in two directions. Understanding is developed as the mind takes in sensory data and ideas. It is deepened as the mind uses new data to modify what it has experienced and processed.

The intellect also works in the other direction as it stimulates and directs behavior. What Gardner (2000) calls the application of understanding is the second intellectual virtue of Imagination. The mind takes in sensory data to develop understanding, and it expresses that understanding as it imagines new actions and possibilities. People whose intellects are alive with new ideas and possibilities demonstrate the virtue of Imagination. They are intellectually competent because their imaginations enable them to take a broad range of actions. Sternberg (1996) called this "successful intelligence."

Two Character Virtues

The virtue of Strong Character is like its common use. It is the capacity to stand for what is right and good in the face of situations and desires that oppose what is right and good. Public schools promote this virtue in several ways. First, the "hidden" curriculum requires students to do homework, meet deadlines, and be responsible. As students confront these requirements, they build character strength by increasing their capacity to delay gratification, cooperate with others, control impulses, engage in unpleasant activities, and accept responsibility. Similarly, the "extra" curriculum promotes strong character by requiring students to train hard and commit to the goals of various after-school activities.

Courage is the other character virtue. The six-virtue definition borrows from Peck (1978, p. 131): "Courage is not the absence of fear; it is the making of action in spite of fear, the moving out against the resistance engendered by fear into the unknown and into the future."

As with all virtues, courage is taught through modeling. When teachers talk about trying to improve instruction, their stories are about taking action "against the resistance engendered by fear into the unknown and into the future." Teachers model courage as they try new things without knowing if they will work.

According to Palmer (1994, pp. 27–28), courage starts with an inward journey that confronts the fears we have about ourselves. When teachers tell their stories, they are not likely to describe an "inward journey" that requires them to overcome fears about themselves. Instead, their stories describe how they moved "out against the resistance engendered by fear into the unknown and into the future" (Peck, 1978, p. 131).

Two Spiritual Virtues

The six-virtue definition of Generosity coincides with everyday use, so little needs to be explained here. Many educators model this virtue. They are drawn to service in schools by their generous spirits, and this is modeled in their daily interactions with students. Undergraduate teacher candidates consistently report that they want to become teachers to give back to others. Similarly, graduate students aspire to join school administration because they want a career that serves teachers, parents, and students.

Of course, not all educators are generous, and generosity is not the norm in all educational organizations. But educators who lack generosity are unhappy in their careers, and organizations where generosity is not the norm are dysfunctional. For the most part, instructional personnel model and teach the generosity that makes educational institutions functional. This modeling provides students with many opportunities to experience the beauty of a generous spirit.

The philosophical meaning of Humility conflicts with popular notions. In popular use, pride is a virtue and being humble is being lowly, but those definitions fail to take into account that pride is the first of the seven deadly sins, and that Jesus was a model of humility, not pride.

In the six-virtue definition of the educated person, Humility starts with knowing one is good. Only those with true gifts and talents can demonstrate virtuous humility. While humble people know they are good, they also realize that others care little about their goodness. They don't brag because, in the face of indifference, bragging would make them look foolish. Furthermore, secure in the knowledge of their goodness, they don't need a spotlight on their abilities. This enables them to recognize and shine a light on the achievements of others. Finally, humble people know that, the day after they die, the world goes on just as it did the day before. In summary, Humility is a virtue displayed by those who know they are good, who know others care little about their goodness, who recognize the talents of others, and who understand their insignificance in the big scheme of things.

With that definition of Humility, it is difficult for teachers to bring their own goodness to the forefront. That is why Humility is evident in just a few of the stories told in the chapters that follow.

On the other hand, teachers often said they sought to deepen their Understanding of their students' backgrounds and learning. And the way they did that was by asking questions. Every verbalization put in the form of a question is an act of Imagination. The question behind the words was conjured up in the mind of the person asking the question at that point in time in that situation. The teachers' stories often point to their efforts to deepen Understanding and to Imagine how to improve.

Teachers also talked about the Strength of Character (the effort) needed to stay current in their fields and keep up with technology. Their reason for making the effort was to provide better instruction for their students. Therefore, Character Strength and Generosity are often part of their stories.

WHERE DOES THIS BOOK FIT ALONGSIDE OTHER BOOKS THAT TELL TEACHERS' STORIES?

Between this Introduction and the Conclusion, with the exception of a brief discussion of the *Leader in Me* program, readers hear only teachers' voices.

Teacher narratives are in the spotlight, and the analyses following each narrative use instructors' own words.

Although the social science improvement paradigm continues to dominate educator preparation programs, several professors have argued for the value of teachers' stories. Several are listed in the bibliography of the second edition of *The Skillful Teacher* (Brookfield, 2005), a textbook on college teaching. But these books stopped short of calling for a new improvement paradigm. In both *Teacher Lore* (Schubert & Ayers, 1992) and *Teachers' Stories: From Personal Narrative to Professional Insight* (Jalongo & Isenberg, 1995), the authors and storytellers argued for the benefits of learning from teachers' stories. Their language, however, sometimes referred to action research projects and teachers doing their own research.

There is nothing wrong with looking at research results, but an aesthetic improvement paradigm focuses more on what comes from inside the teacher. This quotation from the Preface to *Teacher Lore* (1992, p. ix) illustrates one of the fundamental premises of the social science paradigm—that teachers improve instruction by looking outside themselves.

> Seven years ago several of us, all experienced teachers, gathered to study topics of mutual interest. Our attention frequently turned to the lack of participation of teachers in research about teachers. We could all think of wonderful teachers, teachers who influenced our lives and the lives of others. We wondered: Why weren't these teachers and others like them given a chance to share what they learned from their years of service as teachers? . . . We wondered too: What gives meaning and direction to the lives of teachers? What advice might they offer to others who are teachers or want to be teachers? How could good teachers help us better understand how teaching can be improved?

Throughout *Teacher Lore,* teaching is regarded as an art, but the social science improvement paradigm is assumed to guide improvement.

On the other hand, in the same book, Schubert (1992, p. 10) may have been thinking about a new improvement paradigm, when he wrote:

> Our major hope for this book is not that teacher lore becomes what we say, but that it is a beginning of something larger. Something larger is dependent upon those who read this book. We hope it is a challenge to create a broader and deeper sense of what teaching is and can become.

One purpose of this book is to propose something larger—an improvement paradigm that is aesthetic, instead of social scientific. When teaching is regarded as an art, educators see that improvement occurring in four steps, not one or two. The process starts with teachers looking inside themselves, where they see that something needs to be improved. Second, they look outside themselves to deepen their Understanding. They might discover a new supplemental resource or strategy that a colleague has successfully implemented. Third, they Imagine how they might bring that resource or strategy into their situation. And fourth, they look inside themselves to find the other virtues needed to achieve a more beautiful result. It may appear more complicated—to see four steps, instead of one or two—but all four steps occur naturally when artists seek to improve their results.

The primary difference between the two paradigms is in the respect paid to teachers. Instead of assuming that teachers should do what they are told by consultants, professors, or other "experts," an aesthetic improvement paradigm assumes that improvement starts inside the teacher and ends inside the teacher—with the virtues they bring to learning situations. All this is illustrated in the stories that follow.

Another way this book differs from other books that tell teachers' stories is its focus on instructional improvement. Many other books tell stories about a variety of teacher situations. The improvement focus of this book enables readers to see how teachers thought about and went about improving what they do with students.

In conclusion, this book is based on the idea that teacher stories can show us how instruction is improved. It also illustrates that, in teacher practice, the improvement paradigm is an aesthetic one because teaching is an art, not an applied social science.

Part 1

Chapter 1

Stories from Five Elementary School Teachers

ELEMENTARY SCHOOL TEACHER 1 (KINDERGARTEN)

What do you do to reach your most reluctant learners?

We decide some things at school, and some things I decide on my own. Ten years into my career, one of the decisions my school made was to stop assigning homework to kindergarteners. A lot of people fault that idea, but my biggest epiphany was realizing that everything kindergartners need should be learned in school, not after school.

Now I tell parents that I want them to have fun with their child. I want them to read with their child. I want them to have conversations with their child. The children should just go outside and play, and not spend thirty minutes on a worksheet, or argue about doing homework. In the long run having those conversations and interactions helps their child just as much.

In the beginning, I thought homework was a way to link me with families and students, so I gave homework every day. It might have helped those students who had help at home, but it increased the gap between the most advantaged and the least advantaged students.

When I stopped assigning homework, I thought my students were going to fall behind, but I discovered homework really didn't help. If you look at the data, my class is doing better now than it did before. So, I was completely wrong in my assumption that homework was improving achievement.

I still have strong bonds with my parents, and now I have more open communication with them. They read to their kids. It's as simple as that. With kids this young, just having someone talk to them and read to them—that is powerful. Before, when parents were fighting with their kids, especially the reluctant learners who did not want to hold their pencil correctly, parents were done. They didn't want to sit down and read a bedtime story with their kids, even ones with good intentions. They were tired.

Even in kindergarten, everything we do is data-driven—whether it should be or shouldn't, it is. In the process of changing my approach to homework, I looked at the data and I saw the gap between the reluctant learners and the others. That was the "aha" moment. I realized I needed to do something different.

As simple as it sounds, my decision to focus on the daily instruction in the classroom made a world of difference. It works. This decision evolved over my first five years of teaching. It started out with the "no homework" thing, and it has evolved over the last several years.

For example, in kindergarten sight words are a big thing. We used to send the list home and ask parents to work with their kids at home. Then I would assess them for the report card. Eighty-five to one hundred sight words are a big deal for a five-year-old. For several years I continued to ask parents to help their child with those. It wasn't worksheet homework, but I asked parents to read with their child and practice their sight words.

Over the last eight years I decided to take that off the parents. Now I do simple things to help the students with their sight words. We do four sight words a week. I put them on the hallway door, so every time students walk into the restroom, they read me those sight words and memorize them. Every week we add to it. I still let the parents know which sight words I am teaching. That way it becomes more natural when they are reading a book and the kids point out the sight words, but the parents are not responsible for teaching them. As simple as it is—going into the bathroom and reading the sight words—it has worked. In the past the reluctant learners might know only a few sight words at the end of the year. Now all my kids know their sight words.

One of the other things I do to reach the most reluctant learners is pay attention to the teachable moment. I had a professor in college who emphasized that.

We do lots of district initiatives. I take each one and try to make it my own. If they propose a scripted lesson, I make the script my own. I try to always develop the lesson around the children's interests. It could be dinosaurs or remote-control cars.

And we currently use *Letterland*. It's an old phonics program that has changed over time. When we started with it, I did not like it because I had success with the former phonics program. But the kids love the props and the puppets and dressing up like the letter characters.

So, I just took it, ran with it, and that goes back to doing everything in class. I wanted parents to see what we were doing, without any expectations on them. Therefore, I wrote a play called, "Bringing *Letterland* to Life." It covers a lot of what we teach in language arts. The purpose of the play is to introduce parents to the world of *Letterland* and model a few classroom lessons. We have all the kindergartners and first graders dress up as the characters. And the teachers dress up.

I always taught the A-Z sounds, and that was it. But *Letterland* goes into the digraphs and trigraphs and consonant blends.

For example, for the "ch" sound, there is Clever Cat and Harry Hat Man. But when they get together in a word, Clever Cat is allergic to Harry Hat Man's hat. It makes her sneeze, but he hates noise, so it is a polite sneeze: "ch." So, anytime the kids see those letters it is, "ch."

In the play there is a girl dressed up as Clever Cat, and she has a large C on her shirt. There is also a Harry Hat Man. They come center stage and act out their parts while I tell their story. I also call out a few words like chip and chat. Other characters pop up to spell the words.

Each year we invite the parents in, and the kindergartners and first graders perform the play. The parents love it, but they don't have the stress of worksheet responsibilities. Then we invite all the kindergartners and first graders throughout the district, and it is a big deal.

I am the moderator. I play the character Quarrelsome Queen. She worries about her hair, so she always has to have her umbrella to protect her hair, which represents the silent u. We have to put the Q and u together in words or the queen will become quarrelsome. Now, when I go out in the region after a presentation of the play, children will see me and say, "There is Quarrelsome Queen." I briefly feel like a local celebrity.

That way the parents know what is going on because the kids go home and talk about *Letterland* characters. I want them to see how hard we are working to build those words.

A regional amusement park puts on a *Letterland* theme for six days each spring. I wrote a grant that pays for our students to visit the park during that week. It is a big deal. Of course, the parents are invited, so they become involved in that way, too. I still build those relationships. It is just that I do it in different ways.

- -

Several virtues are evident in this story about how a teacher tries to reach her most reluctant learners.

Understanding:
When I stopped assigning homework, I thought my students were going to fall behind, but I discovered homework really didn't help. If you look at the data, my class is doing better now than it did before. So, I was completely wrong in my assumption that homework was improving achievement.

Imagination:
Over the last eight years I decided to take that off the parents, as well. Now I do simple things to help the students with their sight words. We do four sight words a week. I put them on the hallway door, so every time students walk into the restroom, they read me those sight words and memorize them. Every week we add to it.

One of the other things I do to reach the most reluctant learners is pay attention to the teachable moment. I had a professor in college who emphasized that.

We do lots of district initiatives. I take each one and try to make it my own. If they propose a scripted lesson, I make the script my own. I try to always develop the lesson around the children's interests.

Therefore, I wrote a play called "Bringing Letterland to Life." It covers a lot of what we teach in language arts. The purpose of the play is to introduce parents to the world of Letterland and model a few classroom lessons. We have all the kindergartners and first graders dress up as the characters. And the teachers dress up.

Strong Character and Generosity:
A regional amusement park puts on a Letterland theme for six days each spring. I wrote a grant that pays for our students to visit the park during that week. It is a big deal. Of course, the parents are invited, so they become involved in that way, too.

ELEMENTARY SCHOOL TEACHER 2 (GRADE 1)

What do you do to reach your most reluctant learners?

Reading is my passion. Without being able to read, students will not be successful.

I had been teaching about five years, when I took a Reading Foundations class during the summer. We went into depth about how to find the source of a student's reading problems. Maybe it was phonological awareness, or some other aspect of phonics. When I look back, that made a big difference in how I teach reading.

Our exceptional children's program specialist knew of my desire to help struggling readers, so she got me enrolled in the class. It was intense, and I learned so much that I felt bad for not having this information to use with my students earlier.

Most of the time, reluctant learners are not experiencing success because they don't know what to do, and they lack the skills needed to feel successful. If we meet them where they are and help them be successful, they are no longer reluctant. When I was in college, one of the professors impressed upon us that it doesn't matter what we teach our students if we don't enhance their self-esteem. That really stuck with me.

My favorite place to be as a teacher is on the floor with a small group of students. Teaching the whole class is not my favorite. I do it because I have to sometimes.

When I can be with a small group, I can see exactly where they are in their learning. I can help them more. I can get on their level and see exactly where their problems are.

I love our MTSS (multi-tiered system of support) times because in small groups reluctant learners can feel successful. When they are with the whole class, they realize that others know the answers more quickly, so they don't feel successful. The MTSS time is when we look at data about student levels, and we break them into groups and focus on specific deficits.

I actually took that approach before we called it MTSS. We set aside time each day to focus on specific skills for small groups of students. We now do this for both reading and math.

I learned that a lot of behavior problems in my students arose when a student is not sure about what to do. First graders need someone to be there to tell them, "Yes, you are doing it right."

I look at the data and student learning styles. We use a lot of different resources to determine where students are, but I rely mostly on my observations. When I can sit and listen to them read, I hear where their mistakes are.

We break students into groups based on the skills they need. We use group instruction so that students can move on if they are ready for what follows. Students who need more support get it without feeling, "Oh, somebody is waiting on me."

I use the data, but I mainly use my observations. For example, over the past few years, as part of the Read to Achieve initiative, our state mandated the use of a reading diagnostic tool called mClass. I loved mClass assessments. When we looked at mClass data, it usually matched our observations. This year, the state switched from mClass to I-Station. We went from teachers assessing student reading to students sitting at an iPad with a computer program that assessed their reading skills.

I-Station does not involve teachers interacting with the student. So, especially for children with attention problems, we found that I-Station does not generate accurate results. Some students need a teacher to be with them, face-to-face, like we did with mClass. They lose their focus when they are sitting with an iPad.

Furthermore, I-Station is a timed assessment. So, if a student asks to go to the bathroom, I have to ask, "Did you pause your test?" Many times, my first graders would have just walked away from their iPads, causing them to miss several questions.

8   *Chapter 1*

This year we do paper and pencil assessments to make up for losing mClass. We check things like nonsense words and reading fluency. We can see when a student does not stop at periods, or when a child has an issue with phonics or a different problem. We see what we need to work on with each student.

I mainly try different things to see what works. The biggest thing is to help a child feel good about himself. If they do, they will be engaged.

I am a performer. I dress up to portray different characters. Sometimes middle school students will point to me and claim I have a bossy twin sister because I dressed up as that character, when I taught them several years ago.

I look at research, but I mainly care about what works. I don't have to know about the technical, scientific aspects of the findings. All I need to know is if it works for me and my students.

I choose to use some research-based programs. For example, I use right-brain, sight-word cards. They have the words on the card with pictures and a sentence. Children with visual memory problems find success with those cards. I found that program when I was looking for something to help students with auditory processing problems.

My research leads me to try things to see if they work. I use research-based strategies but the most important research for me is what works in my classroom.

- -

Several virtues are evident in this story about how a teacher tries to reach her least engaged readers.

Understanding:
I had been teaching about five years, when I took a Reading Foundations class during the summer. We went into depth about how to find the source of a student's reading problems. Maybe it was phonological awareness, or some other aspect of phonics. When I look back, that made a big difference in how I teach reading.
When I can be with a small group, I can see exactly where they are in their learning. I can help them more. I can get on their level and see exactly where their problems are.
I learned that a lot of behavior problems in my students arose when a student is not sure about what to do. First graders need someone to be there to tell them, "Yes, you are doing it right."
I use the data, but I mainly use my observations.

I mainly try different things to see what works. The biggest thing is to help a child feel good about himself. If they do, they will be engaged.

I look at research, but I mainly care about what works. I don't have to know about the technical, scientific aspects of the findings. All I need to know is if it works for me and my students.

I use research-based strategies but the most important research for me is what works in my classroom.

Imagination:

I am a performer. I dress up to portray different characters. Sometimes middle school students will point to me and claim I have a bossy twin sister because I dressed up as that character, when I taught them several years ago.

Generosity:

Most of the time, reluctant learners are not experiencing success because they don't know what to do, and they lack the skills needed to feel successful. If we meet them where they are, and help them be successful, they are no longer reluctant.

We break students into groups based on the skills they need. We use group instruction so that students can move on if they are ready for what follows. Students who need more support get it without feeling, "Oh, somebody is waiting on me."

ELEMENTARY SCHOOL TEACHER 3 (GRADE 4)

What do you do to better reach your most reluctant learners?

This story is about an autistic fourth-grade boy. It seemed to me that we were unable to truly determine where he was academically with our usual testing procedures. I always felt that he had more to give than what I could see.

We had to get to the point where he and I were talking the same language. What I ended up doing was finding the things that he liked. Of course, there were a lot of conversations with him and his parents, so we could get an understanding of what he was interested in. With him, although he was verbal, he did a lot of scripting.

If he became upset, he would start scripting. And he had certain programs from PBS (Public Broadcasting Service) that he had watched, and he had learned their script. If he got upset with me, there was one script he would say. If he got upset with someone in the classroom, or if he was happy, he had a script. Scripting was when he had memorized what was in the script of a PBS program—what a certain character would say—and he would repeat it in our conversation.

He used to come sit with me after he ate his lunch. If he was having a really good day, he would smile and laugh with me and he would go through a script. It would be something about the whole potato thing, or the windshield, or about winning a race. But it was always the same one. At first, I thought, "That is really bizarre. Why would he say that?" But once I knew it was a script he had learned, I realized that was how he was expressing his emotions. So, we got through that and I got an idea of how he was feeling.

Then I found out that he liked Eric Carle books. He got to a place where he would draw the pictures of the stories—about the hungry caterpillar or the bear. He even got to the point where he had his signature. So, I thought, "This is it. This is what we need to do."

Eventually, we went a step further. He wanted to know more about Eric Carle. From that point we went to looking him up, finding out information about the author, and that piqued his interest even more. So, he got to where he was trying more and to actually read the Eric Carle books. Once I realized that this is what he really enjoyed, we were able to get more books for him to read. Then he wanted to find out even more about Eric Carle. That is where he was that year.

Although he was below grade level, we could see that he could read. Before that it was, "We are not getting very far? What is going on?" For him, that is what it took. We got him to the point where he was checking out books. When his behavior was a problem, he was reminded that "This is a reward for you."

His parents did that, too. If his behavior was good, at the end of the week his parents allowed him to check out books from the library.

There was a lot of trial and error that year.

This boy is now getting ready for high school. He recently came to me and we had a conversation. When he came back, it was, "Hey, how are you doing." And we had a conversation like one I had not experienced, when he was scripting.

- -

Several virtues are evident in this story about how a teacher tries to reach one of her reluctant learners.

Understanding:
Then I found out that he liked Eric Carle books.
But it (scripting) was always the same one. At first, I thought, "That is really bizarre. Why would he say that?" But once I knew it was a script he had learned, I realized that was how he was expressing his emotions. So, we got through that and I got an idea of how he was feeling.

Imagination and Courage:
There was a lot of trial and error that year.
Generosity:
He used to come sit with me after he ate his lunch. If he was having a really good day, he would smile and laugh with me and he would go through a script.

ELEMENTARY SCHOOL TEACHER 4 (GRADE 4)

Do you have a story about how you created one of the best units in your bag of tricks?

I am currently doing a unit about "America on the Move." And one of the things we do is talk about immigration. It is based around our basal reader, which is the basis for our language arts curriculum. But we often incorporate and integrate other subjects. We've been working on immigration to America for the past couple of weeks.

First, I establish a time period for study. In this unit we are talking about the late 1800s to early 1900s. I went out to find other non-fiction readings to go with the basal. I also found videos of first-person accounts. And I found some literature based on immigration experiences, like *Molly's Pilgrim*, *Night Crossing*, or *How Many Days to America?* and things like that.

I did research in several different libraries. I also had to learn as much as I could about immigration, so I can answer questions and find the best resources for things they will be able to understand. If it is too much over their head, they are not going to get anything from it.

Today I introduced them to an activity where they have a suitcase to pack. "You can only take what fits in a suitcase. What would you take and why?" Now they have a week to come up with what they would take. It is called "My Ellis Island" suitcase project.

I came up with this lesson by listening to the students. We were talking about immigration and they were watching videos, and students said, "They don't have anything. Where is all their stuff?" That told me the students struggled with understanding immigrant experiences. It was so foreign to them.

They think, "Oh my gosh. There were no cell phones." So, we ask, "What would you do" questions. If there were no Nintendo games, what would you do? What would you play?

They say, "I couldn't live without my games."

And I tell them, "Yes, you could. You wouldn't even know they exist."

So, I try to put them in that frame of mind—where you can't take everything you own. You can only take what fits in your suitcase. Fill it up, and you may never see your other stuff again.

I usually don't try to stick to a lesson plan. I use them as outlines. The plan is what I want to do, but it goes a different way, when they ask a question. Some teachers get thrown off and fail to take hold of those teachable moments.

Students in this school have 100% free lunch. Many don't have rich, experiential backgrounds. Even though we have children whose families come from immigration backgrounds, they may not know those stories and they may not remember immigration experiences.

Sometimes finding the materials is difficult, and it is difficult when things I need cost money. And sometimes technology is not working. There is always the danger of technology failing you when you need it. Another difficulty is caused by students not being in school. If they are absent when the unit is building, and if they miss something it is difficult for them to keep up with what is going on.

We are having success with this unit. They are excited about this lesson. Just earlier today, they were talking about kids bathing in the kitchen sink. We had seen and read that in a couple places, and it finally dawned on them that that is really what they did. They could not go and take a hot shower. They bathed once a week in the kitchen sink. It is that kind of thing that gets them.

My students have open hearts. They are very smart. They are inquisitive. They care. I just have to make things relevant to them. I try to have them put themselves in the place of those folks who were coming to a new country. Why were they coming? What would it be like if your parents left a few years before you? What if you stayed back with relatives? What would happen after your parents saved up enough money, and you were going to make the trip?

You are ten years old. You are taking care of your little brother or sister on that ship for three months—until you get to New York and meet up with your parents. How would you feel? What would you do? What would you want to have with you? What would be scary? What would be exciting—especially if you are coming and you don't speak English.

Those are the kinds of things we cover. It is interesting to hear their reactions, to hear their ideas. I make things relevant by talking to them and listening to their responses. I ask, "How would you feel? What would you do? What if? Can you imagine?"

It is hard for all of us to imagine what things were like in the early 1900s. A student might say, "You could make a phone with cans and string." But then I explain that they don't even know what a phone is. They start to get it when we go deep enough into it.

- -

Several virtues are evident in this story about how a teacher created one of the best units in her bag of tricks.

Understanding:
Students in this school have 100% free lunch. Many don't have rich, experiential backgrounds. Even though we have children whose families come from immigration backgrounds, they may not know those stories and they may not remember immigration experiences.
My students have open hearts. They are very smart. They are inquisitive. They care. I just have to make things relevant to them. I try to have them put themselves in the place of those folks who were coming to a new country.

Imagination:
Today I introduced them to an activity where they have a suitcase to pack. "You can only take what fits in a suitcase. What would you take and why?"
You are ten years old. You are taking care of your little brother or sister on that ship for three months—until you get to New York and meet up with your parents. How would you feel? What would you do? What would you want to have with you? What would be scary? What would be exciting—especially if you are coming and you don't speak English.

Strong Character and Generosity:
I did research in several different libraries. I also had to learn as much as I can about immigration, so I can answer questions and find the best resources for things they will be able to understand. If it is too much over their head, they are not going to get anything from it.
Sometimes finding the materials is difficult, and it is difficult when things I need cost money.

ELEMENTARY SCHOOL TEACHER 5 (GRADE 5)

Do you have a story about how you created one of the best units in your bag of tricks?

I spend the first four to six weeks of every school year trying to learn my students' personalities, strengths, and weaknesses. Over the years I have accumulated many different resources for my science classes. I have a large library of online resources, many of which I pay for myself.

My classes are all different. Each one has a personality. Some classes are interested in academic things, others are not. One of my classes is interested in social things. They like video games and things like that. So, I have found that I have to treat every class differently, even though they are the same grade level and looking at the same subjects.

Another of my classes loves to sing. They love to dance. They love to move. So, when they come in, I have activities for them that I will not do with other classes. My academically oriented class will not do the singing and dancing. They will watch. They will read the captions on the songs, but they are sitting and not moving much.

My experiences working in a school that had a grant from the Bill and Melinda Gates Foundation opened my eyes to the importance of knowing which problem-based learning (PBL) activities will interest different students. That is when I started to gather materials so students could have them in their hands for PBL activities.

I realized that, if kids have something tangible to work with, if they have something applicable to the standard they are supposed to achieve, I get much more engagement. And then the vocabulary and the concepts are easy because, if I am teaching force and motion, and students have built a roller coaster, we can talk with great interest about gravity, acceleration, and inertia. They don't know they are learning what they are learning, but if they feel the materials and handle them, they are engaged.

The build-up to any successful unit is the anticipation piece. When I plan to create a unit of science activities, I start leaving the materials on the counter. I don't tell them what they are for. My classroom is a hot mess because I have to provide materials for sixty-five students. As I introduce a unit, it is usually through a conversation.

For example, I will ask, "What do you know about weather instruments?" A high percentage of my kids have never watched a weather forecast. Nowadays, they and their parents pull it up on their phones. So, we start with the basics of a weather map. While I am doing this for the first couple of days, I know we are eventually going to build weather instruments. So, I am putting straws, dixie cups, mason jars, and balloons on the back counter. We make anemometers, barometers, and make-shift thermometers. So, for several days I am just laying that stuff back there. And then I bring in actual weather instruments, so they can see what they look like for real.

And the kids ask, "What is all that stuff for?" And I tell them we are going to make weather instruments. And they say, "We can't make weather instruments" because now they have seen what the real ones look like. Then I bring out the burners because we are going to heat water to create a cloud in a jar. And they wonder, why do we need heat to build a weather instrument? So, those are the build-ups.

We start with an anemometer—something simple. I ask, "What does it look like? What does it do? What do we need? Look at the back counter. What is back there is relatively close to what you see in a real anemometer."

Then we go out the back door for a short field trip. I have my anemometer in my hand and I hope the wind is blowing that day. Even in the lightest breeze, it starts to spin. I ask, "Why is it not spinning fast?" And students reply, "It is not very windy."

Then we go through a series of questions and answers, so they see the function of the instrument. Then we go back to the classroom, where the materials I have gathered are on the back counter. And students start to make the connections between the instrument we just saw, the function it performs, and the inexpensive materials on the counter.

The instrument has to have a base, so some students want to make it with pencils. Some want to make it with pipe cleaners. Some say, "I need a wood dowel." And I say, "We don't have one. What are you going to do?"

That gives them ownership. It allows them to explore. That is the engineering piece. The counter is open to them. They know it. They take what they think they need. If it works, good. If it does not, they return it and try something else. I just set them loose at that point. And I can see different ones take a leadership role.

Sometimes the reluctant learners are the leaders because they aren't worried about being wrong. They just grab everything and put things together. On the other hand, some of the honor roll kids keep asking, "Is this right? Is this right?"

At the end of the lesson, after they have their instruments made, I prop the door open, so they can take them outside and see if they work. I tell them: "If it does not work, problem shoot. Don't come and ask me." That is the problem-solving part. I know that this works with them. Now that we are virtual, there have been several times when students have sent me screenshots of things they built. And parents report that their child likes doing experiments at home.

Several virtues are evident in this story about how a teacher created one of the best units in her bag of tricks.

Understanding:
I have found that I have to treat every class differently, even though they are the same grade level and looking at the same subjects.
My experiences working in a school that had a grant from the Bill and Melinda Gates Foundation opened my eyes to the importance of knowing which problem-based learning (PBL) activities will interest different students.
I realized that if kids have something tangible to work with, if they have something applicable to the standard they are supposed to achieve, I get much more engagement. And then the vocabulary and the concepts are

easy because, if I am teaching force and motion, and students have built a roller coaster, we can talk with great interest about gravity, acceleration, and inertia. They don't know they are learning what they are learning, but if they feel the materials and handle them, they are engaged.

Imagination:

I know we are eventually going to build weather instruments. So, I am putting straws, dixie cups, mason jars, and balloons on the back counter. We make anemometers, barometers, and make-shift thermometers.

Generosity

Over the years I have accumulated many different resources for my science classes. I have a large library of online resources, many of which I pay for myself.

I started to gather materials so students could have them in their hands for PBL activities.

Courage:

That gives them ownership. It allows them to explore. That is the engineering piece. The counter is open to them. They know it. They take what they think they need. If it works, good. If it does not, they return it and try something else. I just set them loose at that point.

Chapter 2

Stories from Four Middle School Teachers

MIDDLE SCHOOL TEACHER 1 (GRADE 7)

What do you do to reach your most reluctant learners?

That question is at the heart of teaching because that is where the challenge lies. That is where the drive comes in. That is where you get your second wind, where you can't give up. You can't let it beat you. You have to accept and conquer that challenge.

I am going to talk about the unit I am currently teaching. It has the theme of "survival." We are using the novel *Freak the Mighty* with my seventh-grade class.

Here is how I do it. My students have an interactive student notebook (ISN), and it is the driving force of my class. For every chapter we read, I model every stage. So, beginning with the very first chapter of the book I guide my students. Before struggling students can write a novel summary, they have to learn how to pick out key facts. So, I model for them a lesson, and I do it with them every day. So, we write down the facts. There were four facts in chapter 1.

One method I use is to read the chapter aloud. I change my voice for the characters. I am very animated and theatrical in my reading of the novel. The second method I use is to model everything I expect from the students. After I model a lesson, the third thing I do is hand them an "exit slip," which is a small piece of paper that assesses a skill. Sometimes I ask a question and I ask students to tell me about the specific skill I am about to teach. It can be about a character or something else in the chapter we are on. Students hand their exit slips to me on their way out the door. I read them right away, and the next day I read them out loud to the class. I do not give student names or shame students. I read them aloud for two reasons:

1. So students realize other students are thinking the same thing.
2. So they get recognized for their ideas.

The exit slip also allows me to pre-assess a skill before I teach it. Every day I give an exit slip that pre-assesses a skill that I will teach the next several days. That enables me to know how to put students in groups. I also use data from summative assessments such as Benchmarks, State Check-Ins, and iReady diagnostics, which tell me what to provide for each student.

I sometimes model using graphic organizers. They aid in processing information for each chapter we read. Graphic organizers are used as a vehicle for delivering the information. The graphic organizers are drawn in the ISN or I copy them on colored paper, and they are glued in. For example, for chapter 1 we wrote facts on a fact chart and for the Introduction we did a character web. For chapter 2 we did major and minor characters and the setting using three-column notes. We listed events for chapter 3 using a bulleted list and below it we created a simple summary using the 5Ws: who, what, where, when, and why. For chapter 4 we did a list of prediction questions and their answers. So, I walk them through the lesson every day, and I model it for them. There is always an exit slip which shows me if they got the material for that day.

There is one very important theme for me, and that is motivation. I use a reward system. As students are answering questions, I walk around and hand out tickets. The more tickets they have, the greater their chance of winning in the weekly draw. And they get very excited about that.

I have a SHOUT OUT area in my room on the wall near the door, so it's seen both while entering and leaving. I celebrate my students this way. I purchase inexpensive cardstock cut-outs in a pack of twelve that say, "Good Job!" less than ten cents per student, and I write the student's name on the front and what was awesome on the back. You would be surprised at how many students flip it over to see what their peer was recognized for.

When you are talking about reluctant learners, struggling learners, many times you are also talking about behavior problems. So, one of the things I do with behavior problems is in my little bag of tricks. It's non-verbal and it's called proximity. Proximity works well. I can just walk up to them, and when I am near them it usually deflates anything that can be happening. A lot of times, if something is going on that I don't like, I don't speak to them at all. I just take away whatever is distracting from the lesson.

I am very firm in my discipline, very firm in my management, so all those things are laid out in the beginning of the school year. "This is how a lesson works in my classroom. This is how I react to something you do."

I also use a discipline system that I am absolutely in love with. It is called "Capturing Kids Hearts," which is a district-wide initiative. I use it with fidelity.

Students are constantly giving me informal, informative feedback. I am building relationships and trust, while giving formative assessments, such as "thumbs up, thumbs down." I say, "Do you understand this? Thumbs up or thumbs down." I also reward students with ticket incentives, and I give verbal praise. If a student comes up with an answer while we are doing the problem, I will put their initial down to give that child credit for their answer. So, what we are doing is building their self-esteem, and they are building trust with me and their classmates. And they are being put out there to be shown that I am really proud of them. And that means a lot to them—just to put their initial right beside that question, it shows—"Hey, I got that right." And then they feel smart. This encourages all learners including those above grade level, on grade level, or below grade level.

I use Capturing Kids Hearts, so I ask questions like, "What are you doing? What are you supposed to be doing? How are we going to get back on track?" I was trained in Capturing Kids Hearts four years ago. I'm currently finishing my sixteenth year of teaching. The past four years have been the easiest because of that program.

If a teacher wants to reach a reluctant learner, they must have a discipline system and a positive relationship in place, so the student can feel a sense of mutual trust. You cannot teach a reluctant learner without that. Capturing Kids Hearts provides both of those things, and a third thing, which is an accountability system for the student.

Another trick is sticky notes. If a student is reluctant to learn while I am teaching a unit, I will write something on a sticky note, and I will place it on that child's desk. The sticky notes can say many different things. They can say, "I am really proud of you. Great job on that question." Or it can say, "I know you know the answer. Why didn't you say something?" Or it might say, "You know Ms. Middle School Teacher 1 is proud of you." Or it could say, "I know you can do this. Get your head up and pay attention." Sticky notes do not have a negative connotation, so they can build a "secret" trust. Students think they are important because they are the only child receiving the note.

One of my other tricks is a lot of communication with parents. I use REMIND and I make phone calls two days a week. I over-communicate because it's necessary. I do a lot to build relationships. My biggest advice to any new teacher is to do the following three things:

1. Make a positive parent contact via email, phone, or text within the first three to four weeks of school. I count open house or any school event as long as I make it a point to seek out the parent and even just have a two-minute conversation. One of the things I do every school year is to have a positive contact with every parent within the first three or four weeks. And for the students who I know have been in trouble, or who

have struggled with behavior, I make that positive contact before the first week. You never know who is going to get in trouble on day 1.
2. Build your circle with your most difficult students. Find your ringleaders. Find your alpha male or alpha female and go after them. Identify them and pursue them. You build your circle with the right people. If I showed you my circle right now, you wouldn't believe it. You build your circle with the kids who are the most influential because it only takes one misbehaving student to derail a lesson. I find those students early. I usually ask before the school year starts—from previous teachers—who those students are. I make contact with those kids before the school year starts. I am kind to those students. I give them a piece of candy or buy them a cookie at lunch. I get to know them in the hallway. I talk to them outside the classroom. I build relationships with them, so I am building a circle. Teachers should be intentional and seek out those students to purposefully build a relationship. Those are the students you want on your side because those are the kids that determine the climate of the classroom environment. And those are the students who need you the most.

   I hear teachers say, "Nothing got taught today, because of discipline issues."

   So, my answer to that is, "Are you building that circle? Are you using a research-based positive discipline program with fidelity? Are you reaching out to the kids that you like the least? Are you being kind, being nice, finding something about them that is nice, that you can pick out? Everybody has something you can pick out that is good." Building that relationship is key. If it is not there, you cannot teach.
3. Another trick that I got from a colleague is to give students little jobs. They can be the passer/collector for handouts, a bathroom monitor, an ISN passer/collector, a line leader/caboose, tech expert, clean-up crew, and so on. Give them jobs to build that relationship because everyone else is going to follow them. We as teachers know it is difficult to teach a lesson when three or four students are creating distractions. I know I am being successful with disruptive students when I see them excited. My best units for them have small groups and hands-on activities. It is not easy. If you look at my job board, you will see that a lot of my reluctant learners are my job people. I give them jobs. I make them feel responsible. I make them feel important. I make them feel like experts.

   For example, I have a reluctant learner who knows how to glue things in her notebook. When another student is having a hard time with that, I say, "Now Suzy—you are the expert. I want you to walk around the room and show everybody else how to do it." Suzy is not going to distract anymore. She has a job to do. That is how I involve her.

I am always moving around the classroom. I am active and always asking questions. I'm always involved in what they're doing. And they know they are accountable to me because I am coming around. My room is neat and organized because my reluctant learners are the ones who do it. They have jobs. And when we are doing a lesson in small groups, the students who would be the most disruptive are the ones leading the group. That is paradoxical, isn't it? You would be shocked at how much students try to learn because they don't want to look stupid in front of other kids.

One of my recent success stories was when I moved a severe behavior problem student to an advanced class. This student is brilliant but does not have self-esteem. Two weeks in and that student has been doing amazing. This morning that student came to me and said, "Ms. Middle School Teacher 1, I am going to tutoring next week." I am telling you, I could not get that child to stay after school for me—ever.

- -

Several virtues are evident in this story about how a teacher tries to reach her most reluctant learners.

Understanding:
There is one very important theme for me, and that is motivation. I use a reward system. As students are answering questions, I walk around and hand out tickets. The more tickets they have, the greater their chance of winning in the weekly draw. And they get very excited about that.
Another trick that I got from a colleague is to give students jobs. They can be the passer/collector for handouts, a bathroom monitor, an ISN passer/collector, a line leader/caboose, tech expert, clean-up crew, and so on. Give them jobs to build that relationship because everyone else is going to follow them.

Imagination:
One method I use is to read the chapter aloud. I change my voice for the characters. I am very animated and theatrical in my reading of the novel.
Build your circle with your most difficult students. Find your ringleaders. Find your alpha male or alpha female and go after them. Identify them and pursue them. You build your circle with the right people.
I am always moving around the classroom. I am active and always asking questions.

Strong Character and Generosity:
One of the things I do every school year is to have a positive contact with every parent within the first three or four weeks. And for the students who

> I know have been in trouble, or who have struggled with behavior, I make that positive contact before the first week.
> I also reward students with ticket incentives, and I give verbal praise. If a student comes up with an answer while we are doing the problem, I will put their initial down to give that child credit for their answer.
> Teachers should be intentional and seek out those students to purposefully build a relationship. Those are the students you want on your side because those are the kids that determine the climate of the classroom environment. And those are the students who need you the most.

MIDDLE SCHOOL TEACHER 2 (SPECIAL EDUCATION)

Do you have a story about how you created one of the best units in your bag of tricks?

I strive to create units of study with high interest and engagement. Special education students often feel stigmatized when they are pulled out of their regular classes. My special education class should feel like a privilege rather than a punishment for not meeting certain standards. One of the best feelings I have is when a student comes to me and asks, "How can I get into one of your classes?"

Students are eligible for special education if they have one of the fourteen federal-defined disabilities. For each student we build an Individual Education Plan (IEP), which I implement in my class. One of my purposes is to get them up to their grade level peers. That builds their confidence in all academic areas. The lessons I create address students' IEP goals. They are aimed at ensuring students are achieving grade level skills.

It is difficult to compete with other classes, where students are surrounded by their peers. When they attend my class, they feel punished for missing their favorite subject or for missing social time with friends. Creating "buy in" is a struggle for me because many students aren't confident they can achieve their academic goals. This creates student frustration toward the subject being taught in my class. In other words, sometimes it is stigmatizing for my students to receive the services they need.

Finding materials for reluctant, struggling readers can be difficult, too. It is important to build background knowledge and to find a topic that intrigues the students.

I love my dogs, and I talk about them in class. My students know my dogs by the end of the year because I use them in numerous teaching situations. It is not uncommon for former students to visit my room and ask how my dogs are doing. Most students have had a pet or know of a friend with a pet, which helps bring forward a lot of background knowledge. Students are comfortable sharing their pet stories or their desire to have a pet, which builds rapport within the class.

This project came to light a few years ago when the students read the story of Balto, and they wanted to learn more about dog sledding and the Iditarod. The class begins learning background knowledge about the Iditarod race one month ahead of the actual race.

We begin by reading a below grade level book about Balto to learn about The Great Race of Mercy, which took place when a diptheria outbreak occurred in Nome and medication could not be delivered due to snow and weather conditions. A dogsled relay saved Nome by delivering the medications. The Iditarod Race commemorates this historic dog sledding relay and the importance of dog sledding in Alaska. We then read articles about Balto and the dogsled relay to Nome. Did you know he has a statue in Central Park and is stuffed and able to be seen in the Cleveland Museum?

We then read *Stonefox,* a book about dog sledding whose main character is a young, determined boy about their age. This gives them more background knowledge about dog sledding and cold weather. A student once asked if we could read more books about dog racing because *Stonefox* was the best book he ever read. That is the best comment a teacher can hear from a student who struggles in reading.

Once the background knowledge has been completed, the class begins research on the Iditarod. As an educator, I join http://www.iditarod.com annually. My class creates a huge project based on the information found on this website.

To begin, students research each musher and decide who they think will win this year by looking at past races and the experience of veteran mushers. Students then create a trading card using researched facts and a photo of their chosen musher. Each day students log in to http://www.iditarod.com, and they follow their musher along each checkpoint of the trail. Students record the time the musher arrives at the checkpoint, how long they rest, if they dropped any dogs, and the time the musher leaves the checkpoint.

They can also watch 2–3 minute video clips of their musher coming through each checkpoint. Those videos are interactive and keep the students engaged with the project. After watching the videos, the discussion begins: "What are they asking the mushers, why do you think they are asking this? What is their bib number? What is the number of dogs? Is the musher planning to stay or go?"

Based on what happens in the race, we make inferences and predictions on whether the musher will continue on or rest at the different checkpoints. You should hear the students commenting in class. "Oh my gosh, I dropped a dog. I wonder why they did that?"

I say, "I don't know. Can you look on the site and see any articles about why that might have happened?" The students really invest their time and want their musher to win the race.

Another interactive aspect of the website is the GPS feature. The students can follow their musher in real time using different map views. One view shows the terrain or elevation, and another shows a flat view which is better to see the distance traveled and the distance left to travel. The GPS feature also shows how far ahead or behind their musher is from the other mushers. Students will then document and graph the temperature at the musher's respective checkpoints using positive and negative numbers. Students will find the average temperatures and the range and median of their temperatures, after their mushers complete the race.

As a class we read through the rules of the Iditarod and "What a Musher Must Carry." For our project, students create a picture booklet including those items along with a vocabulary booklet utilizing Iditarod terms such as gee, haw, swing dogs, and Burled Arch.

The race continues for about ten days, which is when the winner arrives in Nome. Students must then research entry fees and prizes. One of the awards, the Red Lantern, is awarded to the person who comes in last. Taking the lantern down from the Burled Arch, which is the finish line, signifies all racers are safely off the trail. This gesture nods to the history of dog sledding because back in Balto's time, each town station had a lantern outside its door to help the mushers safely find its location. Students also read about all the awards given to the mushers. Another award, the Leonard Seppala Humanitarian Award, is voted on by the mushers and vets and awarded to the musher who exhibited the best dog care along the trail. Students love when their musher wins an award and prize money.

This project is reading intensive. The struggling readers find it very difficult to read all the articles online. As a teacher, I have to research ahead of time and pull information from many different sources. One particular article I found and that has an easier readability is about Nelson Stewart, the main trail vet. The article breaks down the responsibilities of each volunteer vet. Dr. Stewart describes the four things vets complete at each checkpoint: hydration and heart, aptitude and attitude, weight, and lungs. Students create a colorful chart with the acronym H-A-W-L for their project. The H-A-W-L chart details what each vet needs to check on each dog at each checkpoint. Each musher carries a yellow vet book along the trail. The vet book must have signatures from the vets along the trail to verify each dog was checked over at each checkpoint.

For teachers, the website has an educational tab with numerous lessons aligned with grade levels and subject areas. I mostly utilize these lessons to give me ideas on how to incorporate the skills I need to teach my students.

One example I use is the Iditarod Checkpoint Multiplication. This assignment lets students assume the vet's role as they take the responsibility of following the dogs throughout the trail. For each checkpoint, the students are given a problem such as multiplying to determine the number of paws the vet will need to inspect for cuts if fourteen dogs enter the checkpoint.

Students have fun being the "vet" through all the checkpoints. I am modifying the math problems this year to correlate with the sixth grade curriculum and IEP goals. The questions this year have decimal numbers, ratios, and percentages:

Welcome to the McGrath Checkpoint.

1. Mushers have 620 miles left to arrive in Nome. What percent of the race have the mushers completed?
2. If a musher pays 2,800 dollars for 120 booties, what is the unit rate?

It is important to individualize the Iditarod project for the grade level and skills of my students. Each year, I add and take out different parts depending on the group of students and their needs.

Overall, students must complete a checklist of items each day once the race starts. Students graph the temperature of the checkpoint closest to their musher. They add data to their musher statistics such as the time at the checkpoint and the dogs dropped. Students also complete a grammar daily edit and two math problems, all with Iditarod themes.

Time management is vital. Students have only forty minutes in my classroom. It is imperative to have every aspect of the lesson planned out, and students need easy access to resources that are on their level. By the end of the Iditarod Unit, students have created a three-panel poster project with all the Iditarod information they acquired throughout the race.

The first year I did this project was at an elementary school and the principal asked, "What are you doing? The kids are running down the hall to get to your room. I have never seen anything like it." I knew this was an extraordinary project when I saw the reaction of my students and the reaction was noticeable from others in the building.

That is the challenge for me—to create something that makes students excited, instead of, "I can't believe I am getting pulled for extra help with reading or math. I hope nobody sees me." Unfortunately, students are very aware in middle school if they are behind. Many would rather hide from help, rather than risk peers knowing they are behind.

One of the appeals of this lesson is that it is a race, which creates some competition among students. I have done other hands-on projects, but this project in particular grabs the students' attention because it deals with dogs and competition. They will say, "I checked on my musher last night and he was resting." They want to see the end of the race and who wins. When their musher scratches or something happens, they take it personally. Students want to learn more and there is a plethora of information at their fingertips.

I am always looking for units to engage my students. If I find something to pique their interest, they will be active participants and want to learn more. I have to weave their individual education goals into high interest activities and projects to get the most out of our time. With the Iditarod, although students identify closely with their musher, the end result is not a reflection of the student's ability. The musher is going to do what he does; therefore, if the musher doesn't do well, it is not a direct reflection on the student's ability.

Whereas if it was a classroom competition and the student had to sit down or be eliminated because he/she missed the question, the student feels like he failed, and everyone knows that. In the Iditarod project, a student will say, "Aw man. My musher scratched." It is important to them, but it does not injure their self-worth or embarrass them. Students want to continue reading and researching to see who wins.

Having fun while learning is like the saying by Confucious, "Choose a job you love, and you will never have to work a day in your life."

Several virtues are evident in this story about how a teacher created one of the best units in her bag of tricks.

Understanding:
Unfortunately, students are very aware in middle school if they are behind. Many would rather hide from help, rather than risk peers knowing they are behind.
With the Iditarod, although students identify closely with their musher, the end result is not a reflection of the student's ability. The musher is going to do what he does; therefore, if the musher doesn't do well, it is not a direct reflection on the student's ability.
Whereas if it was a classroom competition and the student had to sit down or be eliminated because he/she missed the question, the student feels like he failed, and everyone knows that. In the Iditarod project, a student will say, "Aw man. My musher scratched." It is important to them, but it does not injure their self-worth or embarrass them. Students want to continue reading and researching to see who wins.

Imagination:
It is important to build background knowledge and to find a topic that intrigues the students.

For teachers, the website has an educational tab with numerous lessons aligned with grade levels and subject areas. I mostly utilize these lessons to give me ideas on how to incorporate the skills I need to teach my students.
It is important to individualize the Iditarod project for the grade level and skills of my students. Each year, I add and take out different parts depending on the group of students and their needs.
Strong Character and Generosity:
As a teacher, I have to research ahead of time and pull information from many different sources.
Time management is vital. Students have only forty minutes in my classroom. It is imperative to have every aspect of the lesson planned out, and students need easy access to resources that are on their level.

MIDDLE SCHOOL TEACHER 3

Do you have a story about how you created one of the best units in your bag of tricks?

I teach math and science. In science we teach the respiratory and circulatory systems. I teach the basics of how they work together. I give them the basic knowledge first. Then I take gym tape and I tape a heart on the floor. They work with a partner to do a race that shows how the blood moves from the heart into the body, into the lungs, and then back to the heart.

And I make it a race because I have found that middle school students become more engaged if I make it competitive. I stole this lesson from my supervising teacher when I student-taught. The main thing I did to adjust it to my classroom was that I made it competitive.

When I started teaching ten years ago, technology was not what it is today. But I also had developed exercises with Ed Puzzles because kids like video games. So, I followed up Ed Puzzles with how the respiratory and circulatory systems work together.

Between the notes they take, the games they play, the online piece, and the readings we do, the race with their partner is one of the two things they remember when they leave science. The other is dissecting frogs, which I tie in with this unit. We look at the frog heart, lungs, arteries, and veins. When we dissect the frog, they see how it all works together.

I see the technology part as reinforcement. Students need constant reinforcement. So, I am teaching the same material four different ways. I am trying to reach all different learners—the auditory, the visual, the kinesthetic. Reinforcing the same information in different ways is what gets them engaged and interested in learning it. I am going to hit one of the ways they learn during that unit.

I had an activity on my desk for the day we were going to come back from the weekend, but we did not come back (because of the Covid-19 virus). It was an organ application sheet, where they had to pretend they were applying for a job as an organ in the body. I was going to have them use that because it asks, (1) Does this organ work full-time or part-time? (2) Explain why. (3) Who else does it work with? That activity will be one that we do next year. The students will try to prove to the human body that their organ was needed and why it was needed.

As far as math is concerned, I take worksheets, cut the problems out, and paste them around the room. And that gets them moving. It does take extra work, but to them it is fun because they are up and moving. I realized that middle schoolers need to get up. I can't expect them to sit all the time. They are twelve and thirteen. I can't sit all day, either. So, I watched my supervising teacher do a couple of activities that got students up and moving, and I thought, "We can do this with just a little extra effort."

Another thing we do in math is with a new technology tool. It is called "Go Formative." I came across it in the last three years. A lot of times, as a math teacher, you send kids out to do a worksheet on their own—to see what they know. And then they do fifteen problems the wrong way. That means that the next day you are trying to back up and re-teach them. You are doing double-work—trying to undo what they taught themselves—and teaching them the right way.

One of my colleagues heard about this program and shared it with me. I fell in love with it because we can use it during virtual learning days (because of the Covid-19 virus).

My fellow math teacher and I upload a worksheet and put the answers in, so they can see if they are getting right or wrong answers. So, if they do Number 1, and they get it wrong, it says, "You got it wrong."

I use "Go Formative" a couple ways. Students can see if they got it wrong, and they can go back and fix it. But reluctant learners might not take that upon themselves. With them I use the program by sitting at my computer in front of the room (when students are in attendance). I can see that Johnny got six problems wrong. So, I will say, "Johnny come up here. Let's see what you're doing wrong."

I can get them started the right way and work with them, so they are not teaching themselves the wrong procedure. And I can assist the reluctant learners and see the ones who are struggling.

I think the biggest help with developing a bag of tricks is collaboration with other teachers. Our school district is really big on Professional Learning

Communities (PLCs). When one of us in our PLC learns something, we come back and say, "Look at this new thing I learned."

I recently went to a technology conference and came back and said, "Look at these cool things I learned how to do. Look at this new program." There is no point in us reinventing the wheel. We can collaborate with each other. I will say both my PLCs (math and science) are amazing. We are not afraid to share.

When I first came into teaching, it seemed teachers were hoarding things. They sometimes made things they did not want to share. Just in the last ten years, it seems we have made a complete turnaround. Now it is like, "Why don't you take a piece and I will take a piece, and we will work on it together. Being able to collaborate and share what we have helps all of us put more things in our bag of tricks. We can all re-invent and tweak it for our purposes.

Several virtues are evident in this story about how a teacher created some of the best units in her bag of tricks.

Understanding:
I use "Go Formative" a couple ways. Students can see if they got it wrong, and they can go back and fix it. But reluctant learners might not take that upon themselves. With them I use the program by sitting at my computer in front of the room (when students are in attendance). I can see that Johnny got six problems wrong. So, I will say, "Johnny come up here. Let's see what you're doing wrong."
I think the biggest help with developing a bag of tricks is collaboration with other teachers. Our school district is really big on Professional Learning Communities (PLCs). When one of us in our PLC learns something, we come back and say, "Look at this new thing I learned."

Imagination:
I have an activity on my desk for the day we were going to come back from the weekend . . . It was an organ application sheet, where they had to pretend they were applying for a job as an organ in the body.
I am trying to reach all different learners—the auditory, the visual, the kinesthetic. Reinforcing the same information in different ways is what gets them engaged and interested in learning it. I am going to hit one of the ways that they learn during that unit.
Being able to collaborate and share what we have helps all of us put more things in our bag of tricks. We can all re-invent and tweak it for our purposes.

Strong Character:

As far as math is concerned, I take worksheets, cut the problems out, and paste them around the room. And that gets them moving. It does take extra work, but to them it is fun because they are up and moving.

Courage:

We can collaborate with each other. I will say both my PLCs (math and science) are amazing. We are not afraid to share.

MIDDLE SCHOOL TEACHER 4

Do you have a story about how you created one of the best units in your bag of tricks?

One successful unit with my seventh-grade students is microbiology, specifically "cells." This topic can be complex for seventh graders. The first thing I do is build upon their background information and introduce the unit by having students read an article on Jennifer Strange, a young person who died tragically after becoming involved in a radio show contest.

I try to make what we are learning relevant, so students are interested in the unit of study. In this particular unit, we start by reading and discussing the Jennifer Strange story. I show a YouTube video of the radio contest she participated in. She entered a contest called "Hold Your Wee for a Wii." Contestants went to the radio station and drank as much water as they could in a certain period of time without going to the bathroom. The winner would receive a "WII" game system. Basically, as a result of her participation, Jennifer Strange's brain cells swelled, and she died. This captures the students' interest so that when I begin teaching cells I have them engaged in what they are learning.

I begin by teaching the cell membrane. I introduce vocabulary: semipermeable membrane, diffusion, osmosis, plasma membrane, and so on. Students then complete a lab that is commonly used to learn the function of the cell membrane. They use electronic scales to mass a raw egg. They put a given amount of vinegar into a graduated cylinder and then gently place their egg in a jar and pour the vinegar over it. The next day, students remove the egg from the vinegar, realizing that the vinegar has dissolved the shell and that the egg is visibly larger. Students mass the egg again, concluding that the vinegar has moved into the egg across the membrane of the egg.

Next, they place the egg in a jar and pour a given amount of corn syrup over it. On day three, students take out the egg and notice that the egg is smaller and "shriveled" and that there is more liquid inside the jar. Students, again, mass the egg and measure the liquid. As we discuss their data, students are able to determine that the vinegar moved from the egg into the jar. Students are able to realize that, in the case of Jennifer Strange, her brain cells had swollen because water moved across the selectively permeable membrane and into the cell.

This lesson seems successful because of the discussion and questions we have after the lab. For example, one girl wanted to know, "How do I know if I am drinking too much water?" By the questions they asked and the dialogue we had within the classroom, I saw that students understood the concepts being taught. When you make lessons relevant and conduct hands-on activities, they can see and experience the concept. It is no longer abstract.

After this hands-on experience, we learn about more cell organelles using interactive notebooks, graphic organizers, analogies, and more hands-on activities. The students that I currently teach in eighth grade have been able to recall material learned from that microbiology unit in grade 7. My most successful units are those in which we begin with something that captivates and engages my students in what they're learning.

Several virtues are evident in this story about a successful unit in this teacher's bag of tricks.

Understanding:
I try to make what we are learning relevant, so students are interested in the unit of study. In this particular unit, we start by reading and discussing the Jennifer Strange story.
When you make lessons relevant and conduct hands-on activities, they can see and experience the concept. It is no longer abstract.
Imagination:
In this particular unit, we start by reading and discussing the Jennifer Strange story. I show a YouTube video of the radio contest she participated in.
After this hands-on experience, we learn about more cell organelles using interactive notebooks, graphic organizers, analogies, and more hands-on activities. The students that I currently teach in eighth grade have been able to recall material learned from this microbiology unit.

Chapter 3

Stories from Eight High School Teachers

HIGH SCHOOL TEACHER 1 (BIOLOGY)

What do you do to reach your most reluctant learners?

I have always taught inclusion classes, which are classes that enroll students with Individual Education Plans (IEPs). I have students who have been viewed as having a hard time learning, and not being able to grasp all the material. We are kind of expected to pass them anyway. And that wasn't good enough for me. I never liked the idea that some kids could, and some kids couldn't. My job as a teacher is to make sure all kids get it. And I just never believed that students with IEPs couldn't learn the same material as kids who did not have one.

When I started changing the way I approached my most reluctant learners, I had about twenty students. Approximately half were identified as having special needs and IEPs. I had coworkers ask, "Are you going to have two different curriculums?"

I replied, "No, because they all have the same standards. All kids need to learn it." Several coworkers said, "Good luck with that."

So, I just decided that I was going to have the same level of expectations for all the kids and give them all the same work. I knew I was going to have to do some different support and modifications, but that is part of being a teacher. It was a biology class, which they have to pass to graduate. And I never liked the idea of kids not learning biology and still graduating. We were all going to learn biology. That is how it all got started for me.

I started by overhauling my grading system. I moved from traditional grading—A, B, C, D, F—to standards-based grading.

I had a co-teacher that semester—a veteran special education teacher—to assist with implementing student IEPs. We worked together to change everything to a model focused on whether or not kids were learning. If they were not learning the first time through, we had to re-teach. There was a lot of re-teaching. There was a lot of addressing topics in different ways, using different ways to assess kids. We did a lot more one-on-one with students. And we allowed students to pick which of three things they would do. And I geared all that to cover things in different ways—some for auditory learners; some for hands-on learners.

I talked to all the kids. For those who were used to not doing well in school, I told them, "That is not an option anymore. We are going to make sure you learn it." And there was some resistance early on. But once they realized that I believed in them, and I believed they could do it, it was amazing how that changed their perception of themselves.

We changed to a grading scale of 0–4. A big part of it is changing kids' psyches and their belief in themselves. A lot of those kids were getting 30s on papers and tests. If the best is 100, it seems daunting to get from 30 to 100. What really helped kids get it was seeing that, if they got a 2 out of 4, they could see that they were close to getting a 3, which was where we wanted them to be.

That really helped students at the beginning. They were not getting those incredibly low scores anymore. And that helped things shift in our classroom—to where they thought they could do it. We had some kids who had been told they could not do it. And we were determined to prove that wrong.

We just never let the kids get by with not doing the classwork. It was just expected that they were going to do the work until they got it. It was amazing to see these kids, who were used to not being successful, start being successful. And once they started getting 3 or 3.5 out of 4 on things, it was like their whole demeanor changed. That is when I realized we were doing things wrong for a long time.

That was a big part of how I changed what I did. Traditionally grades are given for worksheets, lab write-ups, quizzes, and tests and that sort of thing. Standards-based grading asks, "Why am I grading those kinds of things? If a student did not do their homework, should that really impact their grade?" A lot of our kids live in poor economic conditions. They work after school or have child-rearing responsibilities. There is not much time at home for them to do schoolwork.

So, I look hard at why I graded things. "What were those grades telling me?"

I discovered that when I had given grades in the past, I had kids who didn't do anything in class and did not do any homework, but they aced the test. They were learning it, but they were not showing it in class. I had other kids who did all their work, got A's on everything, but failed the test.

That is when I decided, "This is not working." Certain students needed to get just a few questions right, which was a good accomplishment for them.

I looked at everything and asked, "Are they learning it?" If they were, that should be reflected in their grade.

Having a co-teacher was helpful with this new approach. It gave me confidence to do it. She was like, "Let's see if it works. If it does not, that's okay."

I had been bothered for a long time with the idea that we had to adjust things for kids with IEPs. Now I say, "I don't care. We have to teach them. It is fine with me."

She helped me learn that kids may need a read-aloud for a test. Some may be dyslexic, but that has zero bearing on whether they can learn the material.

One of the biggest things I have changed was talking to kids about their belief in themselves. I did the teaching, reviewing, testing thing, but the biggest change has been me getting to know the kids by asking, "What is your belief about yourself?"

When I started asking kids, "Do you think you can do this?" a lot of them said, "No. I never passed science in my life." That was an eye-opening thing for me. These kids did not believe in themselves, so that changed how I would speak to them. I would say, "If you don't get it this time, we are still in the learning process. We are going to get it next time. I pretty much stopped saying, "You got it right, or you got it wrong." It became more of, "You are almost there. Let's get this covered. We are almost there together."

It definitely changed how I spoke to students. To this day, I still talk to them one-on-one much more than I used to. I ask, "How do you feel about this material? Where are you stuck? If you have had science class success in the past, what is your belief in yourself about this?" If you don't understand where they are, it is hard to reach kids.

I think it has worked for me because I no longer allow myself to think about which kids have IEPs and which do not. In the past, I tried to be more aware of student IEPs, or I knew about a difficult home life; and then I would cut them a little more slack. I stopped doing that.

Now I push everyone toward the same rigorous expectations. I just stopped looking at kids as different, based on what someone told me they could not do in a classroom. Now I believe every kid that walks in can do it, which is how I have been looking at it since that semester. It has worked out well.

I don't put a lot of merit in test scores because they are just a snapshot of where students are, but we have seen significant improvements lately. Scores have skyrocketed, which I think is due to me holding all kids accountable for learning the material. I just make sure all kids get it. I don't believe all kids can't get it.

There are kids I have heard about—who have been in in-school suspension a lot—and I will see their name on the roll in the summer, and I say, "Oh! I've got one of those kids." But I hold all of them accountable from day one.

I don't let them put their heads down and try to hide their earbuds. I just don't let them do it.

It is like, "Nope. You are not going to do that in here." Kids quickly realize, "Oh crap. I am going to have to do work in here."

And they know that I believe in them. If they are out for ten days for out-of-school suspension, and they come back, I tell them, "You have a lot to do. Let's go." It is important for kids to know that you love them and believe in them, and then they really do rise to the occasion.

One of the other teachers said to me, "All your kids are getting it? How is that possible?"

Well, that is the only option I give them. There are some really tough ones. There are some kids who definitely push me. We talk about our kids as some who are "skill" kids and some are "will" kids. Some kids struggle because we have not given them the skills yet. And that is a lot easier to fix than the "will" kids, who have the ability, but who choose behaviors that get in the way of learning. Those kids are the toughest to crack. That is where the one-on-one comes in. We pressure them and give them praise, which helps pull them through.

There is no kid that I have never gotten through to, but some are more challenging than others. Again, I hold the rigor high, saying, "We are going to get this done."

Several virtues are evident in this story about how a teacher tries to reach her most reluctant learners.

Understanding:

We changed to a grading scale of 0–4. A big part of it is changing kids' psyches and their belief in themselves. A lot of those kids were getting 30s on papers and tests. If the best is 100, it seems daunting to get from 30 to 100. What really helped kids get it was seeing that, if they got a 2 out of 4, they could see that they were close to getting a 3, which was where we wanted them to be.

It definitely changed how I spoke to students. To this day, I still talk to them one-on-one much more than I used to. I ask, "How do you feel about this material? Where are you stuck? If you have had science class success in the past, what is your belief in yourself about this?" If you don't understand where they are, it is hard to reach kids.

Imagination:

That is when I realized we were doing things wrong for a long time.

That was a big part of how I changed what I did. Traditionally grades are given for worksheets, lab write-ups, quizzes, and tests and that sort of thing. Standards-based grading asks, "Why am I grading those kinds of things? If a student did not do their homework, should that really impact their grade?"

Strong Character and Generosity:

I have students who have been viewed as having a hard time learning, and not being able to grasp all the material. We are kind of expected to pass them anyway. And that wasn't good enough for me. I never liked the idea that some kids could, and some kids couldn't. My job as a teacher is to make sure all kids get it.

I knew I was going to have to do some different support and modifications, but that is part of being a teacher.

Courage:

I talked to all the kids. For those who were used to not doing well in school, I told them, "That is not an option anymore. We are going to make sure you learn it." And there was some resistance early on. But once they realized that I believed in them, and I believed they could do it, it was amazing how that changed their perception of themselves.

We had some kids who had been told they could not do it. And we were determined to prove that wrong.

HIGH SCHOOL TEACHER 2 (BIOLOGY)

What do you do to reach your most reluctant learners?

When I changed my practices, I saw that my Occupational Course of Study (OCS) students, who I thought were not able to learn certain things, were able to learn them. So, I shifted my beliefs. The first belief I had to shift was that I had to believe students can learn. The second belief was that, if they were not learning, I needed to change what I was doing so they could.

I was taking a course for my master's in school administration, and it made sense to focus on student learning instead of teaching. Standards-based grading makes sense because it is focused on student learning. It shifts the conversation from compliance to what is being learned.

After learning how standards-based learning works, I talked with the other biology teacher and said, "Let's do this." The first shift we had to make was to allow students to be re-assessed. Each assessment is based on a standard. The first thing we had to do was shift from a 0–100 grading scale to 0–4, with Level 3 being proficient.

So, we had to take our assessments and decide what Level 3 was going to be for the standard. When a student was not proficient, it was our job to re-teach them and re-assess them. That was the biggest shift in the classroom.

For a typical high school biology class, you teach the lesson, you give them a test, and if students are not successful, you move on to the next unit. The student has to do extra work and/or get help at lunch or after school. Instead, what we did was, when students weren't proficient, we took a whole day in class to re-group students. Those who were proficient did higher order thinking things and enrichment. And those who were not proficient were re-taught in a different way. Then we re-assessed them to see if they got it.

That was the fundamental shift in our practice. The result was that students loved it because it was the first time they were not required to get it in a two-week time span. If it took them longer, that was okay. We all learn at different rates. For example, one of my OCS students was phenomenal at genetics. When he was in the genetics unit, he killed it.

Our new approach changed things for special education students, too. They would normally always be in the special education group. Now, they were sometimes in the enrichment group. It became not about their disability or their label or compliance. It was about their learning, which created equity in our classroom. It wasn't about anything other than, if you get it, fine. If you don't get it, you get more time. It was strictly about student learning.

Some students did not achieve a 3 or a 4 on the first assessment, but that was okay. We re-grouped them, and they received small group instruction during class. If they still did not get it, we have "Smart Period," where they got one-on-on or one-on-two instruction. Every student did not meet proficiency in every standard, but we saw incredible growth in all our kids.

Several virtues are evident in this story about how a teacher tries to reach her most reluctant learners.

Understanding:
Standards-based grading makes sense because it is focused on student learning. It shifts the conversation from compliance to what is being learned.
Imagination:
After learning how standards-based learning works, I talked with the other biology teacher and said, "Let's do this." The first shift we had to make was to allow students to be re-assessed.
Strong Character and Generosity:

So, we had to take our assessments and decide what Level 3 was going to be for the standard. When a student was not proficient, it was our job to re-teach them and re-assess them. That was the biggest shift in the classroom.
Courage:
The first belief I had to shift was that I had to believe students can learn. The second belief was that, if they were not learning, I needed to change what I was doing so they could.

HIGH SCHOOL TEACHER 3 (MATH)

What do you do to reach your most reluctant learners?

I used to teach the advanced math classes, but nine years ago, my principal wanted me to switch to Algebra I. We had a lot of reluctant learners. We had students who were struggling to pass the end-of-course exam, even after taking the course two or three times. He wanted me to teach Algebra I, to see if we could get better results for those who were not passing the test.

At that time, we started a program called "Progressive Algebra." It provides a way to split Algebra I into modules. Then, if a student does not pass a module, we immediately give remediation and help in those areas where the student is struggling. If a student successfully passes the module, we accelerate the student into the next module. So, we are immediately meeting each student where they are.

The first year we did this, our test scores rose astronomically. But that was the last year the state required and tested Algebra I. The state curriculum moved to an integrated series of math classes. And that changed the end-of-course exam. We decided to stay with "Progressive Math," but the next year our test scores flopped. We didn't change our methods and curriculum enough to meet the new math standards.

We learned a lot that year. The exam was totally different, and we didn't cover things in the depth that the new curriculum required. It was all new to us, so we used it as a learning experience. From that point on we have tried different things to engage our struggling learners. It was an eye-opener. We realized we had to change ourselves and our teaching techniques because the state had changed the expectations for math proficiency.

The state changed from Algebra I to Math I, which is a more integrated math class. We found that the end-of-course test required more reading comprehension. We had to go from teaching the basic skills to the application phase. And that was a change for us. It was about eight years ago that we had to really change how we did things. For example, we have now implemented interactive notebooks, with guided notes each day.

Since then, the state curriculum shifted again, but they kept a lot of things. They kept the integrated model, so we still have Math I, Math II, and Math III, with Geometry embedded within those courses.

The main thing that has changed for me over the last eight years is that I have a more "whole child" approach. Rather than looking at my students as a whole group, I look at each child individually much more than I used to.

Before they ever come into my classroom, I study their previous years' records. I study whatever I can get my hands on. I look at the demographics. Where do they live? What are their previous grades? How have they done in all subjects—not just math?

And that helps me because the first day they walk into my room, I already know some background on each student. I know if they have struggled previously. I know if they are typically knocking the top out of things. And that helps me start teaching that child from where they are at from Day 1.

With Math I, it is not a one-size-fits-all approach. I have students who can't add -5 plus 2. And I have some who are ready to be in an honors class. I review as much information as I can get for each student.

We have students randomly placed in the first six weeks of an eighteen-week, ninety-minute class. That is called Module A. We have either two or three sections of Math I during the same period. At the end of the first six weeks, we have proficiency cuts. Those who are deemed proficient go to one teacher's classroom; those who are not, go to another teacher's classroom.

So, we track students after six weeks. And then we do Module B during the second six weeks. Students who start struggling at that point go back to the remedial class to do Module B. We try to give students the interventions they need when they need them. A child might not need interventions for Module A, but they might need them for Module B.

We group students based on where they need to be, not where other teachers or earlier test data tell us where they are. There are a lot of factors to look at when they come to high school. One factor is pacing. Middle school classes are 180 days. A student may have been successful in math there, but they can't handle the faster pace of a ninety-day class.

Or you may have a student who was a C or D student in middle school because they were bored. They come to us, they get on a faster track, they are being challenged, and they thrive in the high school environment. So, we track the kids based on what they do for us, not on what they have done previously.

Another thing I started doing five years ago is individual student conferences. That is one of the best things I have ever started doing to reach my students. During the first six weeks, I meet with every student for a one-on-one conference of approximately five to seven minutes during class time.

It is time consuming, but it is well worth it. We look at their math history all the way back to third grade. We have all those grades on the computer—within the record-keeping, school software program we use.

The students and I can see if they have always struggled with math, or if the history shows something else. And that opens up conversations about, "What happened that made you go from a B to a D that year? What happened to make you go from a D to an A?"

That gives me a lot of insight into their personal background. I might find out that they moved schools six times during middle school. I might find out there was a divorce or the death of a loved one.

I have a huge classroom, so I can call students back to my desk, where we can have those confidential conversations—away from the other conversations of students doing their in-class work. Typically, the one-on-one conversations take place when others are working on a project or a review.

I try to balance whole class instruction with independent work, so I pull kids back to my desk when it is convenient. I prioritize conferences according to student needs. If I am starting to see an issue, I will see that child first.

One of the effects I have seen with this is that it is easier for students to talk with me after their conference. They have been somewhat vulnerable with me—back there one-on-one. It increases the possibility a student will say, "Ms. High School Teacher 3, I am having trouble right here. Can you help me?"

Those conferences are a key to building a relationship with each student. When teachers stand in front of the class during the whole period, there is no way they can get to know each student personally and understand their situations. It helps break down those walls between students and teachers.

Since I started doing the personal conversations, I would say 90–95% of the students have gotten over that wall between teachers and students. It may take longer with some. One conversation does not fix everything for every student, but it is a starting point. It starts the conversation. It starts my understanding of that child. If I start the conversation, it is easier to continue it in the days and weeks to come.

I usually start by looking back to third grade and tracking their grades. Then we go to where they are in my class. We finish by looking at what the student is doing for me. I tell them their current grade in my class and compare it to their past record. It allows me to see if they are improving or if they need something else from me.

Several virtues are evident in this story about how a teacher tries to reach her most reluctant learners.

Understanding:
The main thing that has changed for me over the last eight years is that I have a more "whole child" approach. Rather than looking at my students as a whole group, I look at each child individually much more than I used to.
Before they ever come into my classroom, I study their previous years' records. I study whatever I can get my hands on. I look at the demographics. Where do they live? What are their previous grades? How have they done in all subjects—not just math?

Imagination:
Another thing I started doing five years ago is individual student conferences. That is one of the best things I have ever started doing to reach my students. During the first six weeks, I meet with every student for a one-on-one conference of approximately five to seven minutes during class time. It is time consuming, but it is well worth it.

Generosity:
One of the effects I have seen with this is that it is easier for students to talk with me after their conference. They have been somewhat vulnerable with me—back there one-on-one. It increases the possibility a student will say, "Ms. High School Teacher 3, I am having trouble right here. Can you help me?"

Courage:
Since I started doing the personal conversations, I would say 90–95% of the students have gotten over that wall between teachers and students. It may take longer with some. One conversation does not fix everything for every student, but it is a starting point. It starts the conversation.

HIGH SCHOOL TEACHER 4 (MATH)

What do you do to reach your most reluctant learners?

There are several reasons I focus on trying to reach my least engaged learners. Some are because of my personality, but mostly it is because I teach math. I have always known that many of my students are not going to like math. I get a lot of students who come to me having misunderstandings, or not having enjoyed it in the past. There are a lot of things in math that make people dislike it. Even adults, sometimes, tell me that they dislike math. If I say, "I am a math teacher," they say, "Oh my! I can't believe you would do that. I hate math."

Half the time the root cause of students disliking math is something that happened when they were in elementary or middle school. By the time students get to me in high school, it is, "Okay, I am not good at it. I have never been good at it. And I am content with that."

But for me, that is not okay. I have always enjoyed math. I like the puzzles and I like that there might be different ways to get to a specific answer. I had great teachers and I had not-so-great teachers in math, but that never discouraged me.

For me it was easy and it was what I always liked, but I am constantly bombarded with, "Well, I don't like it. I am done. I am going to shut down. I don't understand it, and I don't want to try to understand it." My least engaged students are the ones who are having those issues.

Recently I switched schools and there has been a change in mentality at my new school. At my previous school, it was, "Pass them along so they can graduate; or just make sure they can pass the final exam, and then it is fine. We just need those test scores."

Now it is, "Meet them where they are and help them grow. Growth indicates their learning and it is the growth that we want to see." The change in schools resulted in a change in purpose, and I said to myself that I want to be part of this—the mentality of meeting them where they are.

We receive students from many different middle schools. (This is a specialty high school.) They all have different math experiences. Even two kids coming from the same middle school sometimes have different math experiences.

This is my second year at this school. I wanted to start out this year really good. I decided each day: first and foremost, teach math. That is what I love to do. But I also want to teach students that:

(1) Asking questions is necessary.
(2) Mistakes will happen.
(3) As long as they try, they have nothing to lose.

Those are the main things I want to hit every day with my students.

That was my plan this year, but that was not how I approached it in the past. Then it was, here it is, and I am here to help. It was less me reaching out and asking for those questions and requiring that feedback.

As we go through each semester, I constantly ask for feedback from them. I ask for questions from them and I want to see them making mistakes. I also ask about their workload. I ask if they understand, if they need more help, if they need extra practice, and overall, how are they feeling about my class and the math skills they are learning.

With this feedback, I am learning about my students and usually it is the ones I don't need to worry about that are giving me the feedback, that are asking questions, that are telling me, "Yes I get it," or "No, I don't get it."

It is those other, less engaged learners that I am not getting that information from in a normal class. So, now I ask for that information on an exit ticket, which I give to every student before they leave my classroom every day. That is one way I am getting them to interact with me, when they don't want to do it in a classroom full of other students.

My least engaged students are the ones that aren't going to readily ask for help or ask anything at all. They are usually the ones who completely shut down. They believe that if they are quiet, they will slip through the cracks and be left alone. Nobody is going to bother them. But, for me, those are the ones that I zero in on even more.

Those are the students I am constantly watching, when we have work assigned in the classroom. Are they doing it? Are they submitting work on time? If not, it is an immediate call or email home. They learn fast that if they didn't turn something in, they get a "Remind" message. That is how I establish contact with parents and students. I even have a Google Voice number, where they can text me. So, we have the ability to stay in touch.

Reaching out this way also means that my planning block is used for individual or small group work with those students who need extra help. I steal kids from their free time. I send them an email the night before and say, "You struggled with this on your exit ticket, so you are going to come in with me for thirty minutes tomorrow morning." We sit and go over questions that any of them had. We re-work the problem and I give them another one to see if they understand.

This would be in a one-on-one or a one-on-five session, instead of a big classroom session. When some of my least engaged students are in smaller groups, they are able to ask questions without the fear of being considered stupid.

I have students from all over the district. Some learned half of the Math I curriculum last year and some barely learned the eighth grade curriculum. The latter group is often less engaged because they didn't understand and they do not want to ask questions.

Using their feedback from exit tickets, I can see where they were making mistakes. Then I encourage them to move forward and ask questions to finally understand a concept. Each day in math class we have to move on to the next skill.

This is a constant procedure with exit tickets, quizzes, or other kinds of formative feedback. I pull kids in every day. This takes away from my planning period, but, at the end of the day, I am able to reach those kids who could not come before or after school. I get them to ask the questions they need to be asking. After a full year with them, I am able to see where they have questions. And the increased communication with their parents lets them know that I am not going to let them sit and get 60s and 70s on things.

As it turned out, the more they engaged, the more they asked questions and the less time they had to spend with me because they were not being pulled into small group sessions and they could use that time for other things.

A lot of them were able to open up more in smaller group settings. I had a student who was in a different class from her friends. She would say nothing in class, but when she would come to a review session with one or two of her friends, she felt more open and less vulnerable because she was with people she could relate to. She saw her friends ask questions, which encouraged her to ask questions.

The other things I try to do to reach my least engaged students are the following:

1. Being available for whatever they need. It could be additional practice because a student did not understand a concept. It could be to assist with a worksheet, with online practice or with an extra video or notes. I ask if they need review sessions before or after school, or if they can come see me during a specific block. Or I ask if they need to Zoom with me on virtual remote days.
2. I send the message that they should let me know what they need. Then it is up to me to follow through on that. I have seen where there are some teachers who might say, "I am here if you need me," but they don't respond to an email for a few days. It lets the students think the teacher does not care, so why should they?
3. I try to be open and vulnerable with them. If I don't know an answer, I will tell them. If I am having a bad day, I let them know. I tell them that we all have bad days. Or, if I make a mistake while we are doing something, I say, "I made a mistake. Please correct me. That happens to everybody and let's make sure we are learning from the mistakes." If I can be open and honest with them, I see that I get it back.
4. I let them know that I am not going to forget about them. I am not going to leave them alone because I have given up. I try to make sure I am not giving up. I tell them they are going to be dealing with me consistently and constantly—all year long, whether they want to or not.
5. I am a teacher who is constantly reflecting. I reflect on what I am doing and what my students are doing. I think about my own experiences with teachers, knowing that some did the same thing every year. They never changed things. You hear about it, and students know, "Okay. I am going to have the teacher who does this every year." My approach might be somewhat routine, but I am constantly getting feedback about what worked, what they liked, and did not like. That is different from, "I just don't like math." I keep asking, "How can I make this better for you? How can I make it better for the next class?"

Several virtues are evident in this story about a teacher reaching out to her most reluctant learners.

Understanding:
With this feedback, I am learning about my students and usually it is the ones I don't need to worry about that are giving me the feedback, that are asking questions, that are telling me, "Yes I get it," or "No, I don't get it."
Using their feedback from exit tickets, I can see where they were making mistakes.

Imagination:
It is those other, less engaged learners that I am not getting that information from in a normal class. So, now I ask for that information on an exit ticket, which I give to every student before they leave my classroom every day. That is one way I am getting them to interact with me, when they don't want to do it in a classroom full of other students.
I am a teacher who is constantly reflecting. I reflect on what I am doing and what my students are doing.

Strong Character and Generosity:
Those (reluctant learners) are the students I am constantly watching, when we have work assigned in the classroom. Are they doing it? Are they submitting work on time? If not, it is an immediate call or email home. They learn fast that if they didn't turn something in, they get a "Remind" message.
Reaching out this way also means that my planning block is used for individual or small group work with those students who need extra help. I steal kids from their free time. I send them an email the night before and say, "You struggled with this on your exit ticket, so you are going to come in with me for thirty minutes tomorrow morning."

Courage:
I try to be open and vulnerable with them. If I don't know an answer, I will tell them. If I am having a bad day, I let them know. I tell them that we all have bad days. Or, if I make a mistake while we are doing something, I say, "I made a mistake. Please correct me. That happens to everybody and let's make sure we are learning from the mistakes."

Humility:
I send the message that they should let me know what they need. Then it is up to me to follow through on that. . . I keep asking, "How can I make this better for you? How can I make it better for the next class?"

HIGH SCHOOL TEACHER 5 (MATH)

Do you have a story about how you create the best units in your bag of tricks?

Math III is material I have taught for about twenty years, so when I think about the steps I take to create a unit, my response goes hand-in-hand with the question about how units evolve. If I pull away from a unit and look at what I have today, compared to what I had years ago, I see that first you have to become a learner.

The best teachers are the best learners because, as a teacher, you have to ask, "What do I have available to go out and engage students and cover the curriculum?" So, early in my career, after going through National Board Certification as early as I could, I went straight into a master's program.

At our regional state university I went through the MELT program, which is Mathematics Education Leadership Training. At that time the person running MELT was involved with Texas Instruments on a program called T^3 (T-cubed)—Teachers Teaching with Technology. So, I got some very concentrated, very detailed training in using technology in education. And that is something that really stuck with me. It has been in the forefront of my endeavors over the years.

In thinking about different ways of teaching, my training with calculator strategies and technology strategies was earlier than some of my peers. I became the learner. I learned the information and with the new information I gained over the years, that is where my efforts evolved.

The training programs have taught me how to utilize the technology in order to increase student learning. I learned some hands-on strategies, some things where you can use manipulatives. I don't look at manipulatives and technology as either/or. To this day, I continue to use hands-on in my polynomial unit.

A classic example is maximizing the volume of a box. Students have a sheet of paper and they cut squares out of the corners and fold up the sides to form an open-top box. They are going to have different volumes, so the question is, "At what dimensions should you cut the squares to maximize volume?"

That manipulative activity is something I have done for years. You can cut it and the kids can see it. It is tangible. But now, with the technology, we can go beyond that and we can take color programs and color applications where we can look and say, "Now let's follow that up and look at it digitally. Let's look at the dynamic nature of the problem." And that is where a lot of the technology has evolved over the years. It makes it easier for students to visualize the geometry concepts that creep into a polynomial unit.

My instruction has become a more complete product due to the influx of technology. And beyond the Texas Instruments technology, there is so much online. And that part is evolving. As a math teacher I have to ask, "Is there something out there that might be even more advantageous?" So, I have to continue to focus on what is out there to meet the needs of my students.

The main thing I have had to deal with is becoming comfortable with the different technologies in this unit. If we are going to have a continuous pursuit of learning, one of the difficulties is making yourself knowledgeable about the new tools available. Many things are online, and I always have to ask, "Do I need to change something? Do I not need to change something?" I never want to change for the sake of change, but if there is something out there that is better, I want that for my students.

That is how things have evolved. It has made units and lessons more difficult. There are so many things out there, so you have to filter to find the right ones that work for you and your students.

I have success with my lessons when I see student engagement. Our high schoolers are technologically literate, but they are not literate with everything that technology is offering. I take those skills they are good at and ask them to use them in ways they have not done before. Social media—they are super good at, but I want them to take this technology and apply it in a learning situation.

Their reactions vary. Motivated students like it when teachers use different strategies to connect with them—using a technology they can relate to and enjoy. But generally speaking, I get higher student engagement using different activities. And higher engagement leads to increased student learning. You are not going to hit all learning styles every day, but utilizing different approaches means you will hit different styles at different points.

The main idea is that, because we have a society that is ingrained with technology and computers, the types of things students will do at work differ from what they were doing thirty or forty years ago. So, what we expect them to do in school should be different, too.

Several virtues are evident in this story about how a teacher creates math units.

Understanding:
The best teachers are the best learners because, as a teacher, you have to ask, "What do I have available to go out and engage students and cover the curriculum?"
In thinking about different ways of teaching, my training with calculator strategies and technology strategies was earlier than some of my peers. I became the learner. I learned the information and with the new information I gained over the years, that is where my efforts evolved.
...we have a society that is ingrained with technology and computers; the types of things students will do at work differ from what they were doing thirty or forty years ago. So, what we expect them to do in school should be different, too.

Imagination:
But now, with the technology, we can go beyond that and we can take color programs and color applications where we can look and say, "Now let's follow that up and look at it digitally. Let's look at the dynamic nature of the problem." And that is where a lot of the technology has evolved over the years. It makes it easier for students to visualize the geometry concepts that creep into a polynomial unit.

Strong Character and Generosity:
Many things are online, and I always have to ask, "Do I need to change something? Do I not need to change something?" I never want to change for the sake of change, but if there is something out there that is better, I want that for my students.

That (new technologies) is how things have evolved. It has made units and lessons more difficult. There are so many things out there, so you have to filter to find the right ones that work for you and your students.

HIGH SCHOOL TEACHER 6 (SCIENCE)

Do you have a story about how you created one of the best units in your bag of tricks?

When I first started teaching, I taught the way I had been taught, which was to lecture and then do a lab to confirm what the lecture was about. I learned well that way. I was a good student and I loved science because I was able to remember things that way.

Early on I became frustrated, though, because I would cover the information and teach the lab concepts, but students were not able to explain what was happening in the experiments. They were going through the motions, but they didn't know what they were doing or why they were doing it. So, I wanted to find out, "What can I do differently so they really understand, instead of just memorizing."

My first year teaching high school was 1999–2000. It was about three years later that I began to search for a better way to teach biology. I teach in a rural high school, with limited science resources and equipment. I saw an email for a program called "Destiny," which was a traveling "lab" program from our state university.

It was an outreach to rural schools. They had a mobile biotech lab that they would bring to schools. It was all set up to do biotechnology experiments. We local teachers didn't have to do any of the laboratory work. Instead, we did the pre-lab part.

Bringing biotechnology resources to our school really caught my attention. I am old enough to remember when biotech was just beginning. When I was in teacher education, we did a few experiments, but I was not yet comfortable setting that up for my students. And our equipment and supplies were limited.

In order for my school to be part of "Destiny," I had to attend a day-long workshop. I didn't really know what to expect, but I was immersed in the learning all day. At the end I realized that nobody stood in front of me and lectured me. No one gave me notes. It was designed so I could figure it out myself with the help of the people around me. That was an epiphany. I reflected on what I did, what I learned, and how I learned it. When I left they gave me a box with a notebook, a lesson plan, and things ready to go. Those were the things we needed to prepare our students before the visit to the mobile lab.

I found out that these experiments were based on the 5Es, an inquiry-based framework. The first E is engage, the second is explore, the third is explain, the fourth is elaborate, and the fifth is evaluate.

I think I heard about the 5E framework in my college science methods classes. When I look back, I see that I was well prepared in my biology content area, but the education component was a side note. I think I was the only biology education major at my university. I didn't really learn how to do different methods, I just learned about different methods.

That workshop was like a light bulb going on, because now I had been through the 5E framework as a learner. And they gave me everything I needed to conduct that same module in my classrooms. I was hooked. I thought, "This may be what I am looking for because the Engagement (first E) was a scenario called "The Case of the Crown Jewels." The crown jewels had been stolen and there was DNA evidence left behind. Our task was to figure out who committed the crime. It was exactly like a CSI episode.

They didn't even tell you what the process was. They gave you just enough guidance to go through the activity yourself. Then the Elaborate was taking the evidence to the bus where students ran DNA samples to find DNA matches with suspects.

We did that as teachers in the all-day workshop. Afterward, they did an all-day visit to my school. On the day of the visit, my students were able to do the 5E activity. As a young teacher who did not really know what I was doing, it gave me a lot of confidence to have the experts there. They did all the lab prep, and they guided my students. I was there to help. Everything was done in one day, and they cleaned it all up and took it away. It was great for my students.

I was excited about the experiment, but I was also excited about this way of learning. Nobody lectured us about how to do the process, and I wanted to solve the problem by figuring it out myself. Now I understood what gel electrophoresis is. I know a lot more about how DNA works. I learned so much from that module.

In order to continue using this "exploratory method" with my biology students, I wrote some grants to add some of the necessary equipment. That particular lesson was about biotechnology. So, in order to do the exact experiment, you need the right equipment.

You can use the 5E model for teaching many concepts in the science curriculum. That one lesson piqued my interest, so I started researching: (1) What is the 5E model? (2) What are the 5Es? (3) How does it work? And I found that the National Institutes of Health had these other free curriculum modules, and I could order them. So, I started using some of the pre-made modules to begin with, until I became comfortable with the process.

Then I read an article from the National Science Teachers Association. It was about the steps you could take to convert your teaching approach from a cookbook approach to a more inquiry-based approach.

One of the first steps was to make labs an exploration at the beginning of the lesson, so students wouldn't know the answers. The lab's purpose was to help them find the answers. Then we would explain the concepts and they would have an experience as a hook that they could connect to the concepts, instead of the other way around.

The AP (Advanced Placement) biology teacher at our high school also received grant money and began to get biotech equipment, too. The mobile lab program has ended, but I gained enough experience doing these kinds of activities that now I can do them myself.

I continue to write for grants that provide the needed supplies. Our district also provides supplies for our biology classes. I hear a lot of teachers complaining about not having needed resources, but I have not had that experience. There is money available, and if you ask the right way and do the right thing you can get it. It seems like things all lined up for this transition to a more experiential, open-ended approach to biology labs.

About fifteen years ago, my district joined with two others and the regional state university to hire science instructional coaches. That turned out to be my job for two and a half years. The new methods professor at the university used the 5E instructional model for all his classes and training. We used that model to help middle school science teachers implement more inquiry-based instruction in their classrooms. So, I was able to learn with them for two and a half years. The methods professor did a summer workshop for teachers from all three districts. I was sort of an assistant to him, so my job was to go into middle school science classrooms to help them use similar approaches.

The summer workshop was voluntary, and everyone had coaches throughout the year. I was the coach for our district. I used ready-to-go modules to help middle school teachers build their lab activities. I would come in and model the lesson with their students or just be there as they used the materials.

I also started my master's program in science education during that time. We studied brain research to discover why this approach worked, and why it helped students learn science better. And the master's professors taught our classes through the 5Es, so I was learning that model as a student.

I really missed the classroom, so I became a little frustrated with the coaching position. I can't control if other people use the lessons or not, so I begged to go back to the classroom. Now I feel that I am a better teacher because of those experiences. Every lesson does not work through the 5Es, mainly because it takes more time to teach that way. Some lessons need more exploration up front, and then we introduce the vocabulary and explain the concepts after they have explored how things happen.

I need to say that my students do well on the end-of-course exam. But I also have students who go off to college and email me about how they still remember some of our science activities. They say, "I can still remember doing this. I am the only person in my college class who understood how to do the lab."

And that may be an even better gauge for seeing that it really works. If they still remember it three years later, then they really learned it.

All six virtues are evident in this story about how a teacher created one of her best units.

Understanding:
They were going through the motions, but they didn't know what they were doing or why they were doing it. So, I wanted to find out, "What can I do differently so they really understand, instead of just memorizing."
Imagination:
That workshop was like a light bulb going on, because now I had been through the 5E framework as a learner. And they gave me everything I needed to conduct that same module in my classrooms.
Strong Character and Generosity:
I continue to write for grants that provide the needed supplies. Our district also provides supplies for our biology classes. I hear a lot of teachers complaining about not having needed resources, but I have not had that experience. There is money available, and if you ask the right way and do the right thing you can get it.
Courage:
And I found that the National Institutes of Health had these other free curriculum modules, and I could order them. So, I started using some of the premade modules to begin with, until I became comfortable with the process.

Humility:

I need to say that my students do well on the end-of-course exam. But I also have students who go off to college and email me about how they still remember some of our science activities. They say, "I can still remember doing this. I am the only person in my college class who understood how to do the lab."

HIGH SCHOOL TEACHER 7 (AP ENGLISH)

Do you have a story about how you created one of the best units in your bag of tricks?

I am going to describe my favorite unit, which is reading and discussing *The Adventures of Huckleberry Finn*. One of the things that we do in this class is focus on how to read rhetorically. How do you sit down with a piece of text and look at it as social commentary? You keep asking what the author intended; so, you are looking at different structures in the text—syntax, diction, or why characters function the way they do, and why the author created these characters to be this way. Most students are not taught to read this way. They are taught to read for entertainment and comprehension. So, when you teach kids to look at a text in depth, it terrifies them.

This is an AP class, but we have open enrollment, so anyone can take the course. So, I have both high functioning students and others who are apathetic—doing almost nothing—not completing work, not doing assignments. I have the entire spectrum.

In this unit we are reading a piece of literature from the 1800s, which is written with heavy dialect. And that completely throws them off. They are like, "I am stopping. I don't understand."

Jim is the slave and he speaks with a heavy Mississippi slave accent. And Huck is an uneducated white boy, and he doesn't speak properly either. So, when you throw a complex piece of literature at them with dialect, it can literally cause kids to shut down.

I have successfully taught this book for four years now, and it always comes down to getting the kids to buy in, especially the kids who are scared, and especially the kids who don't like to read. Buy-in has to be the first thing. If they don't buy-in after the first fifty pages, they probably haven't read those first fifty pages. And I need them to read the whole text, so they are present and conscious for the discussion.

A lot of times buy-in comes as I preface the novel, introducing the characters, and giving the reading strategies they need to successfully read this book. So, I have to do a lot of pre-teaching. I have to give them a foundation.

That is my responsibility—to make sure that everyone can at least enter on an equal playing field.

One of the most successful teaching strategies I have found with poor readers is modeling. I take them through a smaller piece of text, and I will read it to them, pausing after a paragraph or so, and I ask, "What is Mark Twain doing here?" "And why is it that on this first page, Huck Finn is called a poor lost lamb?" "Why, with all the possible metaphors, does Twain decide to open with the notion that Huck Finn is a lamb?"

That is so significant, and it sets up the loss of innocence that is going to occur throughout the book. So, if I can show them how to ask the proper questions as they are reading, and if I can give them those questions and model questioning for them, then they start to buy-in.

And when they realize this is not just a book about an adventure, but it is about how Southern white society got race relations completely wrong, then they can see that Twain satirizes and critiques what the South did. He uses satire to show that Southerners' actions are inhumane and hypocritical. They are not something we should continue.

From there on we get to talk about race and relate the book to current events. And even the kids will bring up things like the Black Lives Matter movement. And they will look at different race relations issues in our community and within our school. Then we see that this author was incredibly insightful. He published this in 1898, and it is still applicable today. That is what gets their buy-in. And they see that this novel transcends time.

That is one of my favorite things because that is what I love about literature. It speaks volumes about humanity, and it is not just a book with superfluous words. Every word is important because we know the author spent lots of time crafting it. And once you get kids to see that, they are like "Wow! this not only has meaning. This matters, and this can show me how to look at the world around me."

So, this unit gives them those tools to not only read but also to start shaping their own view of the world.

The main difficulty I confront is that I use the version that uses the N-word. I have to do a lot of prefacing at the beginning. I have had kids in two different camps. One set really agreed with the authentic language. It made them uncomfortable, so they would not use it when they quoted the book. And then I had other kids who got fun out of quoting the book. They knew that "Hey we are reading this, so I can say it."

So, we actually had to sit and talk about why Twain used this word, and his intent behind it. We also had to discuss why we can't use it the same way. We can't look at it the way he did. We can't say, "Hey, it is just a word, and we are just joking." That is a difficult discussion.

A few years ago I had a group of white, upper-class kids who were offended that we were reading a book that criticized the actions of white Southerners. That was a first for me, and these kids were not respectful in their criticisms of the book. But we were able to talk about how, regardless of political affiliations, we are human beings, and human beings should act a certain way. So, when we go to the quotations where Huck said, "Humans beings can be awful cruel to one another," we were able to self-reflect. So, it actually broke down that barrier. They were like, "Okay, yes. There are some bad things going on."

And they personalized it, thinking, "I am being attacked because I am a Southern white person and this book is criticizing me." Those were difficult conversations.

We had to do a lot of team building within the class. That was the first year I taught the unit, and the class was really diverse. There were several minority students who were highly offended by this one student's comments. And they wanted to rip him apart. And he really didn't care.

Working through these difficult situations is part of the unit. I want these kids to get along and support one another and be a cohesive class. There have been some really uncomfortable conversations, but by the end of the year we were able to say, "We are human, and we make mistakes."

And showing them how to disagree politely and academically was the biggest challenge that year because some students thought, "I am right. You are wrong. I don't have to listen to you."

And this was right after Trump was elected. There were so many tense emotions in the classroom. They are just sixteen and seventeen years, so they couldn't even vote, but they were highly charged. Navigating that was difficult.

One of the things that I like seeing is that the kids start to understand the significance of things. One of the motifs we look at is moral disease. We look at the role of the doctor, and they make parallels with things they see in today's world. Eventually I see how those academic discussions lead to better writing.

- -

Several virtues are evident in this story about how a teacher created one of the best units in her bag of tricks.

Understanding:
A lot of times buy-in comes as I preface the novel, introducing the characters,
  and giving the reading strategies they need to successfully read this book.
  So, I have to do a lot of pre-teaching. I have to give them a foundation.

That is my responsibility—to make sure that everyone can at least enter on an equal playing field.

Imagination:

One of the most successful teaching strategies I have found with poor readers is modeling. I take them through a smaller piece of text, and I will read it to them, pausing after a paragraph or so; and I ask, "What is Mark Twain doing here?" "And why is it that on this first page, Huck Finn is called a poor lost lamb?" "Why, with all the possible metaphors, does Twain decide to open with the notion that Huck Finn is a lamb?"

Strong Character and Generosity:

Working through these difficult situations is part of the unit. I want these kids to get along and support one another and be a cohesive class. There have been some really uncomfortable conversations, but by the end of the year we were able to say, "We are human, and we make mistakes."

Courage:

And showing them how to disagree politely and academically was the biggest challenge that year because some students thought, "I am right. You are wrong. I don't have to listen to you."

HIGH SCHOOL TEACHER 8 (GRADUATION COACH)

As a graduation coach I work directly with at-risk kids. I get to have a one-on-one relationship with them. And, on several occasions, even at the start of the *Leader in Me* program, I would have kids come into my office and struggle with figuring out what is bothering them. But the seven habits line up so they can reach in to each one of them. Eventually we developed a common vocabulary they can use to express themselves in relation to what is bothering them. We can also use that vocabulary to find solutions.

A perfect example is that one of my students (a junior at the time) came into my office and he told me another student had taken his headphones. He was incredibly upset. Heaven knows where he got those headphones or if he would ever be able to get a pair of headphones again.

The student being accused of taking the headphones countered, saying the boy in my office stole his headphones. So, it was the opposite story with both saying the same thing.

And, just by me asking him questions about how he felt, he went straight into the habits. He said, "I know that I seem to be reactive, but I am being proactive by coming to you, before I go to the kid who took my headphones." And that was true.

Habit 1 is "Be proactive." Habit 5 is "Seek first to understand, and then to be understood." So he went straight into that: "I know I need to seek first to understand where this guy is coming from."

All on his own, he figured out that maybe this other kid needed the headphones more than he did. So, within five minutes of basically talking to himself and using the habits, a very reactive young man (he used to get in a lot of trouble) had worked through his problem, using the tools at his fingertips. And he left my office satisfied, believing the other kid needed the headphones more than he did, which I don't even know if it is true.

But it was amazing to watch him use the lessons he had learned to figure out his problem on his own. If it had been before we started using the *Leader in Me* program, I can't imagine how that would have turned out, whether it would have been a fight in the hallway. At that point in time, we had been using *Leader in Me* for four months.

My other example of how this program has been working is with a student in his senior year, now. He is a good student, but he procrastinates. He gets things done at the last minute, so he is very lucky that he is smart.

We have a "Lead" lesson every Wednesday. One of the lessons the teacher was doing was on planning. That is Habit 3, which is "Putting first things first." It is all about having a planner. These are juniors, and not a single kid had a planner. They had their phone calendars, but they did not even use that.

So, the teacher challenged them to buy or get a planner. If they could not afford it, she would give them one. So, this one student decided he would use a notebook as a planner for one week. He found that, in one week, writing out his plans was so helpful that he now carries a planner. I know that is simple, but it was life changing for that kid. He is no longer a procrastinator. He gets his assignments done in the time he puts in. We call it "big rocks." You identify your greatest jobs and then you put your little rocks to the side. Now this student uses that idea all the time.

These are the little tweaks that enable even our most successful students to be even more successful. So, it reaches every kid—from the at-risk to the higher-performing student.

We were trained last summer. The entire school did the seven habits. One of the very first lessons they did with us is called "the circle of influence." I now use this with all my students and my family on a weekly basis.

You draw a circle on a piece of paper; and then, within that circle, you draw a smaller circle. In the outside circle you write all the things that are concerns of yours; everything you are worried about. Then, at the end, you look at the concerns and realize there is nothing you can do about those concerns.

In the center circle you write all the things you can influence—taking care of your health, communicating with your teachers, coming up with a plan. So, you take this very large circle of concerns and you shrink it down and focus on what you can influence. It frees you up from all that stress. It is a really good exercise for anybody who is stressed out as you set aside those things you can't do anything about.

I use this with adults and students. It is really incredible what happens immediately when people do this lesson. You can see it physically reduce the stressors when they realize what little they can control. They realize that if they spent all that energy wasted on concerns they cannot control, and they used even a small amount on what they can influence, it is life changing.

It is really hard to measure actual results of applying the seven habits because the results go with them (students). The results I would see would be reductions in the number of times students come to my office. I would see them less.

And I would see that they are focusing on the things they can control. I would say most of the seniors I work with have been coming to me with fewer concerns because they can process them themselves and they know what they need to do. They know how to set up their priorities.

Now I see them coming into my office with a planner in their hands. They come back to me, and I say, "Okay, what about your circle of influence?" It is neat because they pull out their circle of influence.

I would say I am better able to help students because they understand the role of their circle of influence. When they show up at my office, 99% of the time, the students have a "concern," and not something they can influence.

One of my students had a serious attendance problem. She would miss school all the time and she could not figure out why. We sat down and did the circle of influence, and she realized it was because she was focused on her concerns and not what she could influence. This last semester she had perfect attendance.

Now she is focused on influencers, creating goals based on her influencers, and setting up her time better. She did a 180-degree turn. In the past year she has turned all her habits around. She is a junior now, and on track to graduate.

It is fitting to end part 1, with a story about how *The Leader in Me* program has been successfully implemented in a K-12 school district. *The Leader in Me* program is based on the social scientific research conducted to discover the seven habits of highly effective people. *The Leader in Me* has been developed, promoted, and evaluated according to the assumptions, questions, and knowledge of the social science improvement paradigm:

1. It is assumed that statistically significant, valid, and reliable findings from social science research point to "effective" behaviors, just like natural science findings point to better medical treatments.
2. Social science researchers seek answers to questions about "effectiveness."
3. The knowledge gained from research findings pertains to the dependent variable. Much of the time it is student test scores. To its credit, however, *The Leader in Me* program cites improvements in student behavior reflected in fewer suspensions or fewer behavior problems sent to the principal's office.

This teacher's story provides evidence of the positive behavioral results achieved through *The Leader in Me* program.

It is essential to point out, however, that *The Leader in Me* program and the six-virtue definition of the educated person are based on different improvement paradigms. The six-virtue definition is based on an aesthetic improvement paradigm, which assumes different things, asks different questions, and produces different knowledge:

1. An aesthetic improvement paradigm assumes that humans experience the beauty in situations when they bring Understanding, Imagination, Strong Character, Courage, Humility, and Generosity; and they experience ugliness when they bring the opposite vices of ignorance, intellectual incompetence, weakness, fear of truth, pride and selfishness.
2. An aesthetic improvement paradigm asks which six virtues and which six vices are part of the situation, knowing that some combination of the twelve is always present.
3. The knowledge gained within an aesthetic paradigm is recognizing what is beautiful and what is ugly in one's life.

Results like the ones described by High School Teacher 8 are laudable. It is ironic, however, that hundreds of school faculties have decided to teach seven habits, the second of which is to "begin with the end in mind;" but almost none of those teachers can define what it means to be educated. (Definitions of "schooled" do not count.)

The analysis of this last story in part 1 differs from the analysis of others, which looked at teachers' descriptions of their own behaviors and strategies.

This teacher describes the behaviors of students who have been taught the seven habits of highly effective people. She lauds her students' behaviors because their behaviors are laudable. Do those behaviors also demonstrate the virtues of the educated person?

Understanding:
Habit #5 is seek first to understand, and then to be understood, so he went straight into that: "I know I need to seek first to understand where this guy is coming from."
Imagination:
In the center circle you write all the things you can influence—taking care of your health, communicating with your teachers, coming up with a plan. So, you take this very large circle of concerns and you shrink it down and focus on what you can influence. It frees you up from all that stress. It is a really good exercise for anybody who is stressed out as you set aside those things you can't do anything about.
I would say most of the seniors I work with have been coming to me with fewer concerns because they can process them themselves and they know what they need to do. They know how to set up their priorities.
Strong Character:
So, this one student decided he would use a notebook as a planner for one week. He found that, in one week, writing out his plans was so helpful that he now carries a planner. I know that is simple, but it was life-changing for that kid. He is no longer a procrastinator. He gets his assignments done in the time he puts in.
Now she is focused on influencers, creating goals based on her influencers, and setting up her time better. She did a 180-degree turn. In the past year she has turned all her habits around. She is a junior, now, and on track to graduate.
Generosity:
And he left my office satisfied, believing the other kid needed the headphones more than he did, which I don't even know if it is true.

Part 2

Chapter 4

Stories from a GED Tutor, a Physical Therapist, Two Athletic Coaches, and a Piano Teacher

INSTRUCTOR 1 (GED TUTOR)

This instructor tutors a woman who is preparing to pass the general education development (GED) exam. Her formal schooling stopped at approximately nine years of age.

What do you do to improve your instruction?

I ask for feedback from her. Did she understand? Can she explain how she got the answer for the math problem?

I sometimes use Khan Academy. We watch the video lesson and I ask her, "Are you clear on what you just saw?" I am trying to get feedback once again. Can she explain what she learned in the video? I want to make sure she did not get lost at some point. I am trying to get feedback from her throughout our session.

What is the significance of using Khan Academy, and where did that idea come from?

I just stumbled upon Khan Academy while searching the web. I am always trying to enhance my two-hour sessions with her. I try to have a variety of activities that reinforce a concept in different ways. So, she is going to hear about a math problem from him (Khan) and we will cover those ideas in the books. I use two workbooks.

When I discovered Khan Academy, I watched him present lessons on different topics, and I critiqued his approach and noticed that he started at the foundation, so I liked his methodology.

I also looked for other instructional websites and videos. Again, I critiqued them and discarded them if I did not find them helpful for my student. I tried to put myself in her shoes. I know her education was basically terminated at Grade 3. She struggles with math and English.

I also found Purple Math lessons and worksheets. It is amazing how many different websites you can go to that refer to another site. I like to explore resources that provide lessons, activities, quiz material, etc. I like that she can get practice activities from those sources. I know that repetition and practice are essential to learning. I get practice materials that are already made for me to use with her.

I work out of two workbooks. I am always looking for materials to be used with my student. I also bought her a set of graphing paper, so she can practice in a more visual way. She can plot the things she is learning in the workbooks.

I give her homework that reinforces what we have been working on. Sometimes the homework introduces a new concept. If she does not get the new concept, I help her by talking it out with her. We do it together. She likes the idea of someone working things out with her.

How do you build a better connection with her?

She trusts me as well as anybody could after working together for one year. She told me that, at the beginning, she was anxious about starting our work together. She had personal anxiety and learning anxiety. When she met with me in the beginning, she could tell that I was easy to work with. She knew that I would be understanding and considerate of her situation. Within the first hour of meeting me, she determined that she wanted to work with me.

I learned to listen and observe her. If she expresses a lack of confidence in her abilities, I remind her that she has already come a long way. She should realize there is a big difference between where she was and where she is now.

Finally, before a tutoring session, which is about two hours long, I look at her homework to see where she got things wrong in the previous lesson. Then I address those when we begin a new lesson. I want to establish closure for her before we move on. She is good at reminding me that, "I am not very clear on that. Could you explain that again?"

- -

Several virtues are evident in this story about how a tutor instructs a GED candidate.

Understanding:
I ask for feedback from her. Did she understand? Can she explain how she got the answer for the math problem?
Imagination:
I tried to put myself in her shoes.

I also looked for other instructional websites, other videos. Again, I critiqued them and discarded them if I did not find them helpful for my student. I tried to put myself in her shoes.

Strong Character and Generosity:

I am always trying to enhance my two-hour sessions with her. I try to have a variety of activities that reinforce a concept in different ways. So, she is going to hear about a math problem from him (Khan) and we will cover those ideas in the books. I use two workbooks.

I work out of two workbooks. I am always looking for materials to be used with my student. I also bought her a set of graphing paper, so she can practice in a more visual way. She can plot the things she is learning in the workbooks.

If she expresses a lack of confidence in her abilities, I remind her that she has already come a long way. She should realize there is a big difference between where she was and where she is now.

INSTRUCTOR 2 (PHYSICAL THERAPIST)

How has your physical therapy instruction evolved over the years?

It is an ongoing process. It goes week by week. I am not one of those people who goes home and reads scholarly articles every night, or anything like that, but I am constantly trying to learn new things, whether it is on social media, through publications, or continuing education courses. Especially in these satellite clinics, it is easy to get in a rut and just keep doing the same things over and over.

There are some things we like to do for everybody because it is going to be beneficial. But I never want to give somebody stuff they can do at home all the time because then, why are they paying to come here and see us?

I follow a lot of power lifters, body builders, and doctors of physical therapy. I even look up some chiropractic stuff. There is a really great website called T-Nation. It is based on doctor stuff and scholarly articles and stuff that has been put into practice by these very smart people that have built great businesses and things like that.

A lot of it is meant for body building or power lifting, but I use quite a bit of it in physical therapy sessions. I operate under the stance that everybody needs to get stronger. That does not mean they need to be able to lift 500 pounds, but when it comes to carrying groceries, going up the stairs, getting out of the chair, everybody benefits from getting stronger.

I also try to pick up a lot from other providers. In my role as satellite clinic coordinator, I have been able to go to other locations. I pick up on what other therapists use that patients respond well to.

So, if we are teaching a complicated exercise or something that is simple, but a patient is not getting it, I make note of what works, what kind of tricks we can use to help them understand it better. A lot of times I will pick up on something from another physical therapist and say, "Oh! Maybe that is what I should be using to help a patient understand better."

When I travel around to our other sites, I see therapists that I have worked with before, and some that I don't know well. Gerald, for example, is a new physical therapy graduate, and he does a lot of different things compared to those of us who have been doing this longer. So, I have been learning a lot from him.

One thing is the way he does evaluations. He just comes out and asks his patients, "What are three things that you struggle with during the day? Rate those in difficulty from 1-10." Then he has them rate it again on their re-evaluations.

It is a subjective thing, but it involves the patient by having them be responsive to how we teach them. It keeps them involved in the process.

How do you make better connections with your clients?

When I worked for a different company, we did a mentoring session every Tuesday. A lot of it was about communicating with patients—how we talk to them and how we use that in our job. One of the things was to give an elevator pitch to somebody that we meet. There were different levels. There was a doctor, a truck driver, and a student. And it was basically learning how to speak at that individual person's level.

So, if I have a physical therapy student I am training, I am going to use more medical terminology. If I have a doctor come in, I will use medical jargon, too. But if my client has no medical or exercise experience, I am going to use more general terms, more illustrations, more analogies to help them understand what we are doing.

Asking questions of the patient is really a big thing to make those connections and get them involved. Whether it is physicians themselves, or whether it is PTs, so many of us have this idea in our heads, before the patient even comes in, of what the issue is. And we don't listen to the person.

In my training I was actually taught that people lie. I realize they do sometimes. I was also taught that what they tell us subjectively is not important. What we do in our objective portion of the evaluation is more important. But I don't agree with that at all. I feel so much of what people tell us, and what they are truly struggling with and why they are coming in plays a big role with how they connect with us and we connect with them, and how we make them feel about how therapy is going.

We have all had those doctor appointments where we felt like we were not being heard. So, I always try to ask them at the beginning of every week,

"What did you have trouble with this week? What is going on with your daily routine?"

The whole point is that you have to target these exercises, when you are instructing patients; it has to be for a reason. It is not just, "We are doing this to make your legs stronger." We need to also explain why their legs need to be stronger: "because you are having trouble getting up to the second floor, or you have to get somebody to help you get up off the floor."

One final thing is that I try to reassure people. A lot of pain science teaching now is saying that how we relate to pain is sometimes more mental than physical. The main thing is that I want to make them feel heard and understood. Sometimes I also relate to them through my own experiences and injuries.

I also tell them that there are things they can still do, regardless of their diagnosis. Just because an MRI shows a herniated disc does not mean they are incapable of doing certain things, or they will have that the rest of their life, or they have to limit their activity. There was a great study that showed you can take a thousand major league baseball players with MRIs that showed rotator cuff injuries, but only one-half of them had symptoms.

How do you make instruction simple and clear?

I have been told that I speak too fast. I currently have a patient who is hearing impaired. Normally, she would be able to read my lips, but now that we are all wearing masks, she can't do that. So now she relies on her hearing aids. She tells me that in order to understand, I have to speak slowly, or the words become just a jumbled mess.

So, now I have to be louder and speak more slowly to make sure she understands my instructions. I don't know anything about sign language, but I find myself talking more with my hands—giving instructions with fingers to show two or three sets of the exercise.

Making instruction simpler and clearer also relates to giving instruction at the proper level. Sometimes people come to me and say that the doctor's explanation was so fast and so laden with medical language that they are not totally sure about their diagnosis. So, a lot of times I try to bridge that gap. And I tell them that I don't expect them to understand all the medical terms.

We try to find out if they respond better to verbal cuing, visual cuing, or tactile messages, where we put our hands on them and move them into position. For some patients I can tell them over and over, but if I don't show them the exercise right in front of them or put my hands on them to show them the positioning, they don't seem to understand.

Sometimes, if it is a multistep exercise, you have to break it down for them. Demonstration is another part of that. I try to never have a patient do something that I can't do. I don't want to be like the person in the workout videos barking out orders and not doing the exercises himself or herself.

How do you know your instruction is based on correct principles?

I had a good education in undergraduate and graduate studies. The problem with so many PTs is the same as for other professionals. Just because we learned something a certain way does not mean there isn't new research out there that disproves it. I try to remember that, just because I was tested this way and this is how we learned it, that may not be true anymore.

You really have to separate personal anecdotes and personal experience from the research. You also have to look at research with discernment and understand its goals and parameters. You can find an article to back up anything you want it to. You can also find articles to negate something.

I look at it now like I look at how people ought to consume news. They should have multiple sources. That is why I try to follow several different PTs and different medical providers. I get all those things together, so I can say, "Overall, research shows us that this is the best direction to go."

We haven't done many in-services now that we are fighting Covid, but we are trying to get those back. Our clinic owner wants us to get continuing education credits and take what we learn back to share.

We try not to be stagnant. There are a lot of groups online. We want PTs who have years of experience and have kept up-to-date with the research. I did six different rotations for physical therapy school, so I was able to learn from a lot of different people in a lot of different settings.

When we had an intern with us, we had them do in-services with us, so we could learn the latest research and not get stagnant. The other part of it is that we must have thirty Continuing Education Units (CEUs) every two years. And part of it is that we get credit for having student interns. That keeps us up-to-date, too.

I presented at the sports symposium one year. To make sure I was giving correct information, I had to do a lot of research and dig into the reasons for the tests we were doing before recommending that athletes could return to their sport after injury.

After I gave that presentation, I could bring that information back to others in our clinic and say, "This is the protocol, and these are the tests we should be giving to make sure our patients are safe and ready to return to competition."

Several virtues are evident in this story about how a physical therapist improves instruction.

Understanding:
One final thing is that I try to reassure people. A lot of pain science teaching now is saying that how we relate to pain is sometimes more mental

than physical. The main thing is that I want to make them feel heard and understood.

We try to find out if they respond better to verbal cuing, visual cuing, or tactile messages, where we put our hands on them and move them into position.

I presented at the sports symposium one year, and to make sure I was giving correct information, I had to do a lot of research and dig into the reasons for the tests we were doing before recommending that athletes could return to their sport after injury.

Imagination:

Asking questions of the patient is really a big thing to make those connections and get them involved.

We have all had those doctor appointments where we felt like we were not being heard. So, I always try to ask them at the beginning of every week, "What did you have trouble with this week? What is going on with your daily routine?"

Courage:

In my training I was actually taught that people lie. I realize they do sometimes. I was also taught that what they tell us subjectively is not important. What we do in our objective portion of the evaluation is more important. But I don't agree with that at all. I feel so much of what people tell us, and what they are truly struggling with and why they are coming in plays a big role with how they connect with us and we connect with them, and how we make them feel about how therapy is going.

Humility:

So, if we are teaching a complicated exercise or something that is simple, but a patient is not getting it, I make note of what works, what kind of tricks we can use to help them understand it better. A lot of times I will pick up on something from another physical therapist and say, "Oh! Maybe that is what I should be using to help a patient understand better."

INSTRUCTOR 3 (BATTING COACH)

What is the story behind how your batting instruction has evolved?

I have always been a student of the game because I wasn't extremely strong or fast or talented as a player. I always felt I had to study more, work more. I read Ted Williams' book a long time ago, and I had a really good high school coach for three years. He was one of those rare high school coaches who knew a lot about the game.

He got me started on the physical aspects of where your hands should be or where your elbow should be. He brought my elbow down when I was a senior in high school. Almost immediately I hit some balls that I couldn't believe I hit. I remember that I hit a ball off the left field wall on the first game that I tried his suggestions. I remember standing on second base and looking at him, and I thought, "Wow! I really crushed one." That got me started.

I have a friend from my playing days who is also a big influence on me. He tried to be a pro player but did not quite make it. Instead, he umpired in the pro leagues. Like him, I had to work hard to get my college degree. When we were coaching partners, we would talk about the Ted Williams' and Charlie Lau's theories of hitting.

Many hitters in the Kansas City organization followed Charlie Lau—trying to throw their hands down at the ball. There was no internet then, so we read magazine articles or wherever we could get theories on hitting. I also hung around the local minor league ballpark and worked out with the local baseball guys.

My college coach was very successful, but he didn't teach me anything about hitting. I got more from my friendships with the top baseball guys in town. We talked about Charlie Lau's theories, but mainly about "what works."

So, my evolution as a hitting instructor and coach for thirty-nine years (high school and Legion) is based on being at the ballpark much of the time from March to September. I am kind of a baseball freak. The evolution continues.

I saw Ted Williams speak a long time ago at a national coaching clinic. When I hear somebody who really makes sense, I lean that way, until I hear something else that makes sense. Now I am beyond both Ted Williams and Charlie Lau, and I teach that the shoulders should be parallel to the bat as much as possible. They have a lot of videos that show the barrel of the bat is down, when good contact is made. And it really works.

My evolution comes from what works. I coached a lot of games and held a lot of practices. I see what works, and this newest theory works better than anything I ever taught before. The hands are quicker, so the batter can really drive the ball. I wish I knew about this in my playing days.

I now go to internet sites where I see videos of major league players—any of them I want to see. And they all look the same at impact. They may start with different stances, but when they separate and attack the ball, they all look the same.

I also have changed what I teach about the stride. We hardly stride anymore.

I am just a student of the game. I had to work really hard on the fundamentals. I just keep looking to learn. I check with any instructor I can. I used to go to spring training. I tried to watch instructors to see what they were doing.

I love coaching hitting because there is so much to it. There are so many parts to it. And the kids have to know that you know what you are doing.

Since I played at the college level, I have some credibility with them. Other coaches have even more credibility if they played pro baseball.

What do you do to make a better connection with the hitters you are instructing?

The main thing is to not be critical all the time. My coaching partner is a powerful guy, but I can't be that guy. I am not a dominant boss at my company, either. I am more quiet and laid back. I want to be cerebral. I don't do well when I yell at somebody.

It is easier for me to be that way because I am an assistant coach. It is more. "I am their buddy." The head coach is the tough cop, and I am the nice cop.

So, if a player strikes out with the bases loaded, I won't say anything right away. At the next practice, though, I will get the player alone and ask if he understands what the team needed when he struck out. And we will have a conversation, where I make the point that a ground ball is all we needed to get a run. If he was trying to do too much with a two-strike count, he needed to adjust his mental approach and just try to get the bat on the ball.

Then I will stand by the batting cage and set up that game situation. "Here we are, Joe, bases loaded, no outs. What do you want to do?" Then he practices getting the bat on the ball. And we might go back over that at bat to see what was going through his head. I want them to think more about what they can do to help us win.

What do you do to make instruction clear and simple?

I ran into a former player a while back in the mall. Several years after he played, when he saw me, he said, "Just say no to drugs and high pitches." He remembered that from many years ago. We said that all the time. Even in batting practice, we used to say, "Say no to high pitches."

He remembered that all those years later. Did it work? Maybe. It is a goofy example, but maybe it worked.

How do you make sure your lessons are based on correct principles?

There are so many technical things. You learn what works over the years. Some of the things I have tried just don't work. And some things work for some kids and not for others.

Rhythm is another important aspect of hitting. How do you get that? I focus on how a hitter triggers the approach to the ball. We look for a good timing mechanism.

The stride is another technical thing. I watched one of the other high school coaches teach that the hitter could not stride until he was able to hit the ball without striding. He was teaching how not to strike out.

I have been doing U.S. baseball academy clinics for about twenty years now. We get a bunch of information from them. That is where I learned about getting videos to look at major league hitters' swings. It is just amazing what the swing looks like when you break it down.

This new theory about the barrel below the hands—I never even thought of that until I heard it from Aaron Judge's hitting coach a couple years ago. Now you hear about launch angle, exit velocity, and all that. We started looking at all that, but you have to be careful with high school kids. In the big leagues they want guys to hit home runs. We want young hitters to hit line drives.

For the technical stuff, we keep cycling back to drilling with a tee, with a toss, with sessions in the cage, and with hitting sessions on the field. And after games we come back and evaluate after the emotions are gone.

I want to evaluate players when they are calm, when nobody else is watching, and nobody is being critical of them. I just want to know. "How can we get better together?"

And if they trust me and it works, we are getting where we want to get. We want them to be loose and quick. We want them to have an unrestricted swing but be intense enough to get the bat there in a hurry. That is an unusual combination—being intense without being tense.

Several virtues are evident in this batting instructor's story about how his instruction has evolved.

Understanding:
I read Ted Williams' book a long time ago, and I had a really good high school coach for three years. He was one of those rare high school coaches who knew a lot about the game.
He got me started on the physical aspects of where your hands should be or where your elbow should be. He brought my elbow down when I was a senior in high school. Almost immediately I hit some balls that I couldn't believe I hit. That got me going.
When we were coaching partners, we would talk about the Ted Williams' and Charlie Lau's theories of hitting.
Many hitters in the Kansas City organization followed Charlie Lau—trying to throw their hands down at the ball. There was no internet then, so we read magazine articles or wherever we could get theories on hitting. I also hung around the local minor league ballpark and worked out with the local baseball guys.
Imagination:
That is an unusual combination—being intense without being tense.
My evolution comes from what works. I coached a lot of games and held a lot of practices. I see what works, and this newest theory works better than

anything I ever taught before. The hands are quicker, so the batter can really drive the ball. I wish I knew about this in my playing days.
Generosity:
The main thing is to not be critical all the time. My coaching partner is a powerful guy, but I can't be that guy. I am not a dominant boss at my company, either. I am more quiet and laid back.
I want to evaluate players when they are calm, when nobody else is watching, and nobody is being critical of them. I just want to know. "How can we get better together?"

INSTRUCTOR 4 (GOLF COACH)

How has your golf instructions evolved?

My goal is to have the student do something they did not think they could do or hit a shot they did not think they could hit. As far as the evolution of my instruction, I think I have become more effective at pinpointing the issues that need addressing. This means we have less wasted time and more productive time. When I first started teaching, I would look for certain things, but I was not as good at dissecting what I was looking at. I am much better at that now.

I don't take a cookie-cutter approach to my lessons. Everybody that I teach is a different height, size, and shape. My approach is to teach individuals to get the most out of the unique swing that they have. I am from the old school. I grew up watching golfers like Lee Trevino and Chi Chi Rodriguez—golfers who had different types of swings but who were very effective. When it came right down to it, even though it looked different, all the pieces of the puzzle were connecting when it mattered.

So, I have gotten better at diagnosing my students, better at putting aside the stuff that does not matter. Then I am dialing in on the things that I hope are going to make a difference in their swing. There hasn't been any one thing I see in my evolution, but I certainly have gotten better at dissecting the swing and understanding the key components of what it takes to put my students in the best position to get the best results.

What do you do to make a better connection with your students?

First of all, I like to keep the lesson light hearted. I might even try to make the student laugh a time or two during the lesson. Anytime I am giving a lesson, especially to a new student, there is going to be some nervousness involved. I may not know the person well, but they are going to be performing the golf swing in front of me. It can be embarrassing for them, and it often creates anxiety, especially when they have somebody standing directly in front of them, diagnosing what they are doing.

Second, I want people to enjoy the lesson while we are working toward a goal. I don't want it to be drudgery or like rocket science. So, I try to limit the amount of information I give them and focus on just those things that are most likely to make a difference. I have probably said this a thousand times during lessons: "Just stay loose, don't worry about what you look like and try not to be self-conscious."

And the way that I make them feel at ease is telling them that I have embarrassed myself to death on the golf course. I like letting people know that this is a hard game. It is like playing an instrument. You are not going to pick up a guitar and start jamming the first day you pick it up.

Finally, I sometimes simply have them stand back and I will give them an example, a visual example of what they are doing incorrectly and sometimes that can help as well.

What do you do to keep your instruction clear and simple?

People have different personalities. Some can handle the more technical information, but for others, it blows their mind. I don't want to give a lesson to a person who is doing decently well and then pack them full of so much information that they can't even take the club back. Some people would get bogged down with too much information. I have found that the closer you get to a "scratch" golfer, the more you need to provide detailed information because it can be the tiniest little thing that is throwing off a skilled golfer.

But for the average golfer, complicating things or giving too much information is not a good thing. I try to keep it relatively simple. I stick to two or three fundamental things and work from that point. If the student develops to a point where I can break it down a little deeper, that will be fine.

A beginning golfer is just trying to make solid contact with the ball. That is my thing. I try to get people to make solid contact more times than not, even if the direction is not that great. Golf is so much more enjoyable if you are making solid contact—even if you are a little bit wild.

I try to be realistic. There is no perfection. So, I let them know that I can't line up perfectly every time either, but I am going to try to line up as perfect as I can. And then I am going to go for it. So many times, in sports, you just have to go for it. If you are hesitant, if you decelerate, if there is doubt, the negative aspect of golf feeds on that. I try to keep people positive. So, much of it is a mind game as well. I tell students to trust what they are doing and just go for it.

You have to become a student of the game and to achieve this you must humble yourself 100% to the game and all of its nuances. You have to understand how certain things are connected to produce the desired result. As with any sport, there are some things that have to be done correctly. There are a few "musts" with golf, too. You have to have a good grip, good alignment, and proper ball position.

When it comes to the swing, though, I am careful not to dissect it unless there is a fatal flaw because I believe we all have a different swing and a different personality in our golf game. So, I realize there are some things that need to be in place, but I tend not to re-build a person's swing unless there is a fundamental correction that must be made. From the very beginning I had a natural swing and was able to play this game fairly well, but it was only after I became a student of the game that I was able to truly understand the game and become an effective teacher.

What do you do to make sure your teaching is based on correct principles?

Growing up with golf all around me my whole life, having the opportunity to practice and play with highly skilled players from a young age, I was simply ingrained with the principles of a proper golf swing. Over the years I watched other people play, I watched other swings, I watched instructional videos. I took some lessons and tips from people who have helped me along the way. It is a culmination of many things and experiences that lead up to truly understanding the fundamentals.

One of the first things I do with students on the practice range is to have them pick out a target. I need to know where they are trying to hit the ball in order to know if they are properly lined up with the club, the feet, the shoulders, and everything that needs to be working together. And most of the time what I see is people who think they are properly lined up, but some basic things are way off.

Another thing is ball position. You need to understand the correct ball position with clubs that are of different lengths. And the grip has to be proper, too. It all starts there. All those are the fundamentals I focus on in the setup.

There are also key components of the swing. I look at the swing path. I look at shoulder turn. You have to turn the shoulders, or you have not completed a golf swing. I also help people by teaching them what works and what hasn't worked for me through the years.

Although there are clear fundamentals of the golf swing, I also realize there is no perfection—no perfect alignment, no perfect grip. There is so much going on in the golf swing. Some days you feel comfortable over the ball, and some days you don't.

For me a lot of it comes down to the psychology of sports. So much of it comes down to believing you can do it. If you don't believe you can do it, you are not going to do it. So, I try to stay positive and provide positive reinforcement. If we are on the range and the student hits a good shot, I may give them a high-five. I want them to enjoy the fact that they just did something they thought they could not do. And that might lead to them believing they can do it again.

Several virtues are evident in this golf coach's story about improving his instruction.

Understanding:
There hasn't been any one thing I see in my evolution, but I certainly have gotten better at dissecting the swing and understanding the key components of what it takes to put my students in the best position to get the best results.

Anytime I am giving a lesson, especially to a new student, there is going to be some nervousness involved. I may not know the person well, but they are going to be performing the golf swing in front of me. It can be embarrassing for them, and it often creates anxiety, especially when they have somebody standing directly in front of them, diagnosing what they are doing.

Imagination:
So, I try to limit the amount of information I give them and focus on just those things that are most likely to make a difference.

So much of it is a mind game as well. I tell students to trust what they are doing and just go for it.

For me a lot of it comes down to the psychology of sports. So much of it comes down to believing you can do it. If you don't believe you can do it, you are not going to do it. So, I try to stay positive and provide positive reinforcement.

Generosity:
And the way that I make them feel at ease is telling them that I have embarrassed myself to death on the golf course. I like letting people know that this is a hard game.

Humility:
I try to be realistic. There is no perfection. So, I let them know that I can't line up perfectly every time either, but I am going to try to line up as perfect as I can. And then I am going to go for it.

INSTRUCTOR 5 (PIANO TEACHER)

How has your piano teaching evolved over the years?

My teaching is always evolving as I consider each student. When I am teaching a private lesson, I am teaching an individual who is not going to be like the others I have taught. So, I want to understand how that particular student thinks, how he/she processes things. I have to know the individuals—what kind of unique needs they have, and then my teaching has to be geared to that. So, my instruction will vary from student to student.

Usually, the curriculum I use is consistent between students, and then I adapt it to the student's needs. That is important. I need to spend some time getting to know the student and have conversations with the parent. I want to stay connected to them and convey to parents that I am interested in knowing how their child learns best. Most of my students range from kindergarten age through high school age, with just a few college students.

From parents, I try to find out how their child learns best at school. What interests them? If I find out the student likes jazz music, then I try to incorporate that into the curriculum. Or maybe they like a Disney song, or a popular song, or something they might play in church. Focusing on student interests can motivate them to learn the techniques and skills important for traditional learning. Can this motivate them to learn the music of Bach? I think so and I have experienced that with my students.

As the student progresses, I start thinking about the music they are working on. Is there a diversity of music? Are they playing music from each of the four basic areas of music history? I want to make sure each area is being covered to enhance their knowledge and learning.

In addition to teaching students how to play music, my curriculum covers music theory and history, which is an important part of the learning process. As a teacher, it is important to put in some preparation time outside of the lesson to allow the lesson time to be more productive. As I review the student's progress, it's at that time that I think, this piece by Gershwin has some jazz idioms in it, which are good for the student because of her interest. Or I think about the theory book that has a little extra history that is going to be good for this student.

When I am in the lesson with a student, I might play a couple different pieces and let them choose. "Do you like this one or that one?" This is similar to what I did with my own children. You don't say, "What do you want to do?" You say, "Do you want to do this, or do you want to do that?" And you give them choices you can live with as a parent. That is what I do as a teacher. I give students choices I can live with—choices I know will cover the important things the student needs to learn. That also gives them input into the lesson, which is important.

How do you make better connections with your students?

My students don't come in the door without me asking, "How are you? How was your day? What did you do in school, today?" Again, I treat them like I treated my own children. You have that short window of time, when you pick your children up from school, that you can find out what was going on in their day. Then they are moving on to something else by the time you get them home. That car time was always important to me with my own children.

It is the same way with my students. The first few minutes, when the student walks through the door, I want to know how their day was. That helps me understand if they are going to be in a good mood that day. I read their body language. "What am I sensing here? How am I going to connect with them, if they are struggling?" You can tell when they walk through the door, if they had a rough day. Maybe they had an argument with a sibling or their parents before they got out of the car or perhaps school was especially challenging that day.

So, first of all, if there is any anxiety, or if they are upset, I want to diffuse that. We don't spend a long time talking, but we spend a few minutes just talking and catching up with each other. And then we begin the lesson for the day. And all of that helps me understand where they are. Sometimes we get through it in a good way, and sometimes I realize, "Ok, this is how it is going to be." Then I try to maintain realistic expectations.

Another example of maintaining realistic expectations is happening this week. We are seeing students again, at the start of the new term. You have hopes that the three-week holiday break meant they had time to practice and do grand things while they are away from you. But the bottom line is that they are probably not going to do so much. So, you have to set realistic expectations for each student, knowing what they are capable and helping them realize their potential. You have to keep it real on the grand scheme of things as there is so much that is competing for their time. Piano lessons are just one of the many things these students will be doing over the course of their week. So, I try to keep it real.

In some cases, I have been teaching students for years. It has been rewarding and fun to see them grow. I have had students who went on to major in music in college and then continue in music professionally. It is wonderful to see them have that kind of success.

What do you do to make your instruction clear and simple?

When I start a new piece with a student, I say, "Let's look at this piece and break it down. Where do you find patterns—things that are similar, things that are exactly alike? Things that are different? Do you see repeating sections?" Like anything in life, we break it down. We ask, "What can I do to take care of this today? tomorrow? the next day?" Music is the same way. We might work on the right hand, and then the left hand. Then we put the hands together. We break it down into smaller chunks. And then you realize, "I can be successful, if I break it down." I have found that if it takes too long to explain something, it is probably not the best project or assignment for that student. There may need to be another step added to the learning process. So just like in life, you break it down into something simple. I want to do that with my students.

If we run out of lesson time I may say, "See what you can do on your own with this piece for next week." Sometimes they come back still overwhelmed. Then, when we break it down, that is when you see those light bulb moments. They say, "Oh yea! Why didn't I see that?" They just have to learn to see the smaller parts of it, and then how to put that back into the whole. Those are the special moments, having patience with them and working through the thought process, "Ok, you probably knew how to do that, but you didn't do that, so let me show you how." That is where, as a teacher, you can't get all wound up about it. Again, you keep those expectations real. You have patience with your students knowing you want a long-term relationship with them. You are teaching more than music to your students: you're helping to develop life skills.

How do you make sure your teaching is based on correct principles?

I have had a variety of teachers from the time I was six years old. My mother was also a musician and one of my teachers. One of the things we should do as a teacher is think about how we were taught and try to take the best things from each of those teachers. I read a lot. I have studied various philosophies. I am not a purist of any one educational style. I prefer to incorporate the best of different approaches. And that has helped me develop my own style of teaching.

I believe in what I teach, and I believe it is important to stay current. In the past I have reviewed various curricula, not only for piano, but in other educational areas. We can learn teaching techniques from areas other than our own. I have been a curriculum writer, so I understand the research you have to do to find the resources and studies to be able to write your own curriculum. It is important for teachers to stay fresh, to continue to be creative, and to learn new things.

Sometimes it means going back to an old book that I read in college. That often reminds me of why I do the things I do and why certain methods of teaching have stood the test of time.

I know there is still so much that I can learn. But I have faith in what I do. I feel like what I do is legitimate and fair and right, but I always want to be open to learning from other teachers and professionals.

One final thing I want to say about working with my students is that, for me, it is more about their musical journey than it is about the final product. Of course, I want to see progress. But for me it is about the journey and about their continual learning process. When they are fifty, sixty, or seventy years old, I want these students to be able to sit down at their pianos and play whatever they would like to play. Hopefully we all keep learning. That has served me well in all my years of teaching.

Several virtues are evident in this piano teacher's story about how she improves instruction.

Understanding:
So, I want to understand how that particular student thinks, how he/she processes things. I have to know the individuals—what kind of unique needs

they have, and then my teaching has to be geared to that. So, my instruction will vary from student to student.

The first few minutes, when the student walks through the door—I want to know how their day was. That helps me understand if they are going to be in a good mood that day. I read their body language. "What am I sensing here? How am I going to connect with them, if they are struggling?"

Imagination:

Focusing on student interests can motivate them to learn the techniques and skills important for traditional learning. Can this motivate them to learn the music of Bach? I think so and I have experienced that with my students.

That is what I do as a teacher. I give students choices I can live with—choices I know will cover the important things the student needs to learn. That also gives them input into the lesson, which is important.

So, you have to set realistic expectations for each student, knowing what they are capable and helping them realize their potential. You have to keep it real on the grand scheme of things as there is so much that is competing for their time. Piano lessons are just one of the many things these students will be doing over the course of their week. So, I try to keep it real.

Strong Character and Generosity:

As a teacher, it's important to put in some preparation time outside of the lesson to allow the lesson time to be more productive. As I review the student's progress, it's at that time that I think, this piece by Gershwin has some jazz idioms in it, which are good for the student because of her interest. Or I think about the theory book that has a little extra history that is going to be good for this student.

Humility:

It is important for teachers to stay fresh, to continue to be creative, and to learn new things.

I know there is still so much that I can learn. But I have faith in what I do. I feel like what I do is legitimate and fair and right, but I always want to be open to learning from other teachers and professionals.

Chapter 5

Stories from Two Music Teachers, a Pastor, a Goodwill Trainer, and a Team-Building Consultant

INSTRUCTOR 6 (CELLO TEACHER)

How has your instruction evolved?
When I first started, I had taken one week of teacher training at a Suzuki Institute. Those were long days for a week. I didn't have any confidence because I really did not know what I was doing. So, for quite a few years, I went back to take week-long training sessions every summer. My teaching got better.

Then I had a daughter, and she started taking violin lessons, which was huge learning for me—to see how it works with the parents at home working with the kids. That was big learning in terms of allowing the student to do whatever they needed to do and work with what they had. I realized I could give them positive feedback and ask one little question: Would they like to try something different?

I continued over the years to participate in the week-long workshops and observe other teachers teaching. So, I have learned a great deal for myself in the teacher training workshops. I also learned how different teachers teach on different instruments. That has been huge for me, too.

For the last ten years I have also attended three-day "Tennessee Cello Workshops." That is where famous performers and teachers come from all over the continent. I get to attend lectures and talks and hear them perform. That is all very helpful for my teaching.

I continue to play in an orchestra and do chamber music of many different kinds. Playing and performing has really helped with my teaching as well.

More recently, with the advent of meeting on Zoom, I had to view some YouTube videos to see about the best ways to teach music with Zoom. I have to keep up to date with the latest technology and with what families are using to listen to music.

How do you make a better connection with your students?

I encourage parents to connect with me. Especially if they are having motivational issues, I get them to text me every day. I ask, what did they do? Or, if there is some issue going on, parents can text me, or email me, or phone me. In other words, between lessons I stay in touch with the parent or the student (if they are older). It doesn't involve much time, but I am connecting with them.

Lessons are typically once a week, but twice a month we have small groups, so the kids can play music with each other. It is a little more challenging on Zoom, but yesterday I did some small groups. It motivates them to see each other and to play with each other.

What do you do to make sure your instruction is simple and clear?

There is a very important part of the Suzuki program. I can't remember what it is called exactly—something like, "one point of your lesson." It means you focus on that one point for the whole lesson—make sure they understand it, and then have them use it in all their practice for the week.

And, when there is something new, I make sure we adapt whatever tiny morsels of a new technique or musical language to their ability level. I don't give them any more than they have shown me they can do in the lesson. I want them to solidify and own the new piece before we learn more. That is how they grow. When they feel easy and comfortable with what they are doing, they can grow from there.

How do you know your teaching is based on correct principles?

There are a few principles that are part of the Suzuki method. One is that when they are young, the parents are their teachers at home. I have to make sure the parents understand what their lesson points are for the work at home. There is the Suzuki triangle, which is parent, student, and teacher.

Until they are responsible enough (maybe at ten or eleven years old), it is the parent's job to make sure they are listening to the music they are learning. Daily listening to the music makes it possible to learn to play music, just as we learn our mother tongue—by hearing our mothers speak it.

There is some disagreement in the Suzuki world about reading music. I think there has been a misunderstanding that happened early on with Suzuki violin teachers. They didn't start the kids reading music early enough. We don't usually start reading music until the kids can read books. We do activities with basic music reading skills before they start reading music. So, it is the same principle of tiny steps and making it easy to grasp. We start early with basic skills.

My final thoughts are that I am passionate about teaching, and the passion grows as I get older. I am always looking at the latest books on cello pedagogy and cello performing. I think it really helps if you love playing the instrument and love the kids and want them to have a really good time and grow into loving adults. The most important element of teaching is that you love the kids and love to watch them grow. If you are a music teacher, it also helps to love music.

Several virtues are evident in this cello teacher's story about how she improves instruction.

Understanding:
I had to view some YouTube videos to see about the best ways to teach music with Zoom. I have to keep up to date with the latest technology and with what families are using to listen to music.
There is some disagreement in the Suzuki world about reading music. I think there has been a misunderstanding that happened early on with Suzuki violin teachers.
Imagination:
I realized I could give them positive feedback and ask one little question: Would they like to try something different?
And, when there is something new, I make sure we adapt whatever tiny morsels of a new technique or musical language to their ability level. I don't give them any more than they have shown me they can do in the lesson.
Strong Character and Generosity:
In other words, between lessons I stay in touch with the parent or the student (if they are older). It doesn't involve much time, but I am connecting with them.
I am always looking at the latest books on cello pedagogy and cello performing . . . The most important element of teaching is that you love the kids and love to watch them grow.

INSTRUCTOR 7 (ACOUSTIC STRINGS AND BAND DIRECTOR)

Background

I teach a wide variety of the traditional string instruments that are played in blue grass, old time, and other acoustic music. So, I teach bass, guitar, banjo, mandolin, fiddle, etc. I have approximately twenty-five students during the course of a week. Students usually have one lesson per week with me—either an hour or thirty minutes, depending on their age and ability.

There are several facets to my teaching life because I do individual lessons at an arts academy, and during the summer I teach master classes at music camps. These include week-long intensive study with students on things related to songwriting and music theory, as well as individual instrument instruction.

It is a broad range, and I come at it from two different perspectives, which are the classical music band perspective as well as the oral tradition of the musicians where I grew up. I combine those areas to create my teaching style.

The second style of teaching is what has been passed down through observation and learned by rote. And then I combine that with the liberal arts way of viewing music education and teaching. I had teaching experience in college and in the high school band. After our high school band director had a heart attack and needed time to recover, I became like the band director for my junior and senior years.

It is really hard to separate traditional music teaching from the oral tradition because my style is a combination of both. I do them together.

How has your instruction evolved?

I started giving lessons in the back room of a pharmacy when I was fourteen years old. I knew nothing about formal teaching, but I did know how to break down tunes and break down what I was doing stylistically. It was "I play, and the student plays back," just like I was taught when I was a kid. I listened to the old fiddle players and banjo players from the area, and my learning was completely rote. That was the most basic way I taught. I didn't do anything other than that because I hadn't yet developed my teaching style.

Filling in for the high school band director was important in my development as a teacher. It taught me about the way my emotions came across to students. One of the things I remembered about band directors was that many of them were "yellers." They were not mean, but there was a sense of edginess and emotion when they talked.

One of the things I experimented with in my high school teaching was to go through the range of emotions and to go through the range of being loud and being super soft. I tried to keep changing, so students would stay with me the entire time. I took that idea with me when I went back to giving individual lessons.

From that point on, my individual lessons have been about creating a lesson so the student is with me 100% of the time. And I do that by showing a wide range of emotions. For instance, when one of my younger students comes in, I might not say a single word. Then I will mime what I want them to do. I might mime for the whole lesson.

Or a student might come in and I will play an Ed Sheeran song because I know that kid likes Ed Sheeran. I try to keep an emotional change happening, and I think that was one of the big evolutions from teaching just rote, trying to add varying emotions to what I was doing with my students.

The emotional changes I bring to situations are based on the student's personality, which I get to know through individual lessons. I know how much I can engage with each student without making them feel uncomfortable. It takes a long time for some shy students to get to the point where they are comfortable even talking with me. So, I have to provide emotional space for them to be okay with what I am doing.

Some students are immediately comfortable, so I can immediately tell little jokes and share funny stories. My emotional range—reacting to student personality types—is truly the marriage of the things I learned in those formative years.

How do you make a better connection with your students?

The number one thing from my classical music teaching experience was that I saw many instructors who taught as if everybody was going to be a little Mozart. I use a beach-going metaphor to explain my reaction to that.

My father saw the movie *Jaws* and was terrified of going into the water, but he enjoyed looking at it. My mother could not swim very well, so she put her feet in and walked in the shallows. I like to swim, and I don't care what is underneath me. I try not to think about it. I just swim. And then I have friends who are marine biologists. They want to know the ocean salinity of the Indian Ocean. They want to know the mating rituals of the sea horse. They want to get it all, but they will never get it all. They will only get a small drop of the ocean.

The day I realized that not everybody has to be a marine biologist taught me that, as a teacher, I needed to find out what my students' involvement with music was going to be or what they wanted it to be. Then I should teach that way. I should not prescribe something because I think they should learn it, but I should teach based on what their involvement with music is currently or might be in the future. And then I can sneak in things that might interest them. Waders don't necessarily love the ocean any less than a marine biologist. That's the beauty of the ocean of music.

How do you make your instruction simple and clear?

I am a big fan of checklists for my teaching. My students' attention span and their age affects how much I put on the checklists. Here is an example. When I was teaching marching band, I had to think about what is happening from someone's toes to their head—at any given time. So, I created this system, where I would stop the entire band and say, "Checklist," or say some crazy word that would make them laugh. And they had to go from toe to head. They had to notice everything their body was doing to see if it was what I had prescribed.

When I am teaching fiddle technique, for example, and there are all these things students have to keep in their head—all at the same time—it is really difficult. So, what I do is I figure out what those important things are and I put them on the opening checklist. Then I say, "Go through your technique checklist." And they have to go through it in their own head.

Then I say, "When you are practicing, I want you to go through the technique checklist at least three times in your head." That gets them to ask: Am I standing up straight? Am I holding the fiddle right? Am I holding the bow correctly? Is my elbow up or down? And so on. I go through the checklist with them and the checklist gets added to as students become more adept at what they are doing. So, I do simplification through checklists they can readily recall.

How do you make sure your teaching is based on correct principles?

That is a touchy subject for music teachers because in the music world—whether you are doing teaching, production work, engineering work, or sound work—everybody has their opinion. And everybody thinks their principles are right and other principles are wrong.

So, it is difficult to determine the most important information to share with students. There is disagreement about what should be taught first and what should be emphasized—should it be technique, should it be having fun, or should it be building a large repertoire of tunes?

Here is my response to that question:

I have to teach in a way that meets the student's interest and then expand it. In other words, if I can find what their interest level is in music, then I try to slowly expand it, no matter how I have to do that. Maybe they like rock and roll or Korean pop—whatever they are interested in. And then they learn that Korean pop was influenced by a scale found in traditional Korean music. Then they say, "Oh, that is why these notes are here."

So, first I find their interest. Second, I find a way to expand their interest. Third, I find a way to allow music to draw them out into something that is bigger than what they viewed it in the larger scheme of worldly experience. In other words, I know one of my students is not going to be a professional musician. But I also know that student has a musical ear and is capable of having a good time playing in a weekend band. I might get that student interested in arranging so he/she can become a leader in that band.

The last thing is realizing that it is better to be on an equal footing with my students, rather than them feeling like I am dictating to them. I do this in performance all the time. I became a better performer when I stopped thinking of the audience as my audience, and I am performing for them. Instead, I started to realize that what I had to do was draw them in, so it is like we are all on the front porch, playing fiddle tunes with the sound echoing off the back of the mountains, like in my childhood.

I want it to be like we are not doing a lesson. We are just getting together so student and teacher can play music and have fun learning together. They are learning about music from me. I am learning about teaching from them. Those principles are my biggies. Everything else is extra.

Several virtues are evident in this music teacher's story about how he improves instruction.

Understanding:
I knew nothing about formal teaching, but I did know how to break down tunes and break down what I was doing stylistically. It was "I play, and the student plays back," just like I was taught when I was a kid. I listened to the old fiddle players and banjo players from the area, and my learning was completely rote.
The day I realized that not everybody has to be a marine biologist taught me that, as a teacher, I needed to find out what my students' involvement with music was going to be or what they wanted it to be. Then I should teach that way.

Imagination:
One of the things I experimented with in my high school teaching was to go through the range of emotions and to go through the range of being loud and being super soft. I tried to keep changing, so students would stay with me the entire time. I took that idea with me when I went back to giving individual lessons.
For instance, when one of my younger students comes in, I might not say a single word. Then I will mime what I want them to do. I might mime for the whole lesson.
So, what I do is I figure out what those important things are and I put them on the opening checklist. Then I say, "Go through your technique checklist." And they have to go through it in their own head.

Generosity:
The emotional changes I bring to situations are based on the student's personality, which I get to know through individual lessons. I know how much I can engage with each student without making them feel uncomfortable. It takes a long time for some shy students to get to the point where they are comfortable even talking with me. So, I have to provide emotional space for them to be okay with what I am doing.

INSTRUCTOR 8 (BAPTIST PASTOR)

How has your instruction as a pastor evolved?

After graduating from the seminary in 1980, I spent six and a half years pastoring in a small town in Virginia. My next position was at a university campus church for eleven years. From there I moved to a suburban church, which is where I serve, today.

My first pastorate was at a church that had a custodian and a volunteer secretary. Other than me, that was it.

In terms of the technology we used, although I had not seen one in years, this church was still using an old, hand-cranked mimeograph machine. I felt like an astronaut compared to where they were. So, I helped them move into using a copy machine. Why I remember this, I don't know, but the AB Dick copier we bought was able to put out a "stunning" six copies per minute. And we thought we had moved into the space age.

Coming back I can tell you that teaching in the church is always about getting to know the people well enough to know the questions they are asking. Then, if you are trying to influence them in the long run, you need to give them something they can hold in their hand. So, hard copies of the things I would be teaching were essential.

By the early to mid-1980s, personal computers were coming along, but I still did not have one. We were a small-town church, and we were still operating in a simple manner. That was fine with me because my teaching approach always started with knowing who it is that I am teaching.

I left that church in 1986 and moved to a church on the campus of a university. While I was there, I got a computer and became part of the computer age. And I loved it. But what was the same was the teaching approach. I had to get to know the people I was talking to. But other things were different. It was a different kind of knowledge than what I needed before.

At the small-town church we had two hundred people. I knew all of them. I knew where they lived. I knew when there was a graduation. Generally, I knew when there was an anniversary. And I always knew when there was a death.

But in the university community I was actually pastoring three churches—the student church, the faculty and administration church, and the church for the neighboring community. Suddenly, it was not as easy to know the people I was teaching.

It was a good stretching experience. I am so grateful for it. With the college students changing every year, I had to learn what college students in general were asking in addition to what a particular college student was asking. Where are they going? What is at the core of who they are?

And once again, it was the personal, face-to-face where I was most effective. What I noticed in the transition was that, by the time the mid-90s got here, a lot of the things I had been doing started to take different forms.

I had been invited year after year to be among the camp pastors at state assemblies. And there would be several hundred kids there and I did not know any of them. That opportunity went away because I aged out. They wanted to get younger pastors, but it also happened that the number of people going to camp diminished. It is not that they were not interested in learning. It was that they were not interested in learning that way. So we had to find modules that would work in a local setting.

The end of the story for me is that I have been at a community church for more than twenty years. I am facing retirement in a couple of years, and I have watched technology pass me by. I can't keep up with it. I tried vigorously and failed. Eventually, I realized I was trying to keep up with technology, but people were not asking technological questions. They wanted to know things of the heart and how the heart and mind work together to produce meaningful faith.

When I look back at it now, I realize that is exactly what they were asking in 1980, when I began my pastorate. It hasn't changed any. The good news for me is that I now serve a church that has four associate pastors—a pastor of students, a pastor of families, a pastor of creative worship, and an associate pastor. They are all wonderful, and they are also technologically savvy.

So, when I need to bring technology into the teaching, they help me do that. They make me look pretty good, when the reality is that I don't have a clue how those things work. I just know that they do.

I have discovered that my lack of technological knowledge has never become a factor for most of the congregants. They are looking for a personal connection. They are not looking for me to replicate what they experience in their technological world. So, for me, what I was certain would be something that would drive me away from the teaching experience has not done that.

For those who know me well, I struggle with deeply conservative Christianity. I think it has done damage to the Gospel and done damage to people because it has tried to give hard, fast, unchangeable answers to the questions of life that are never hard, fast, or unchangeable.

When some people hear me appeal to the heart and brain, they sometimes find that to be a turn-off. They want me to say, "This is what it is and this is what you are supposed to believe. And if you do not believe it, you need to get yourself in line and believe it."

But I found there is a much greater thirst among people who say, "Teach me how to think about the first five books of the Old Testament, when it talks about creation and the instigation of the nation Israel, and the Flood story, and the Exodus. Teach me how to think about all of that. What is really going on there?"

When you set them free to do that, their theology is going to be an ever-evolving thing. I am not saying the God they are in love with today is not there anymore. I am saying their theology becomes a magnetic thing, so they are drawn nearer to God as they have freedom to ask hard questions of scripture.

How do you make your instruction clear and simple?

What I am discovering is that some people had been told, "believe this" and they tried it. Often, it failed them. What I want them to do is what the Apostle Paul said, "Work out your own salvation—fuss with it, fight with it. Do all you can to make your salvation meaningful to you." If all a person does is accept what somebody else said, I am not sure how meaningful that can be.

We like to travel. We love the national parks. We took a tour of the Grand Canyon, and I am guessing that tour guide mentioned 500 facts about the Grand Canyon in two and a half hours. And I can't remember any of them, and yet it was the greatest tour I have ever taken because, as I was hearing his stories about the things we were looking at, I was not caught up in his words, but in the experience of what I was seeing.

The one thing I remember was a story he told about a kid whose mom and dad took him out west.

> They said, "Tomorrow, son, we are going to the Grand Canyon." And he said, "What's that?" They said, "It's a beautiful cut in the earth. It is a mile deep." The next night they saw him writing in his journal. When he was sleeping, they picked up his journal to see what he wrote. After seeing the Grand Canyon he wrote, "Today, I spit a mile."

I remember him telling that story. Why? Because I was standing there at the edge, looking into the canyon. And all of a sudden, I realized, "I want to know that kid."

Maya Angelou reminds us that, "It is not a matter of what someone tells us or tries to teach us, it is how they make us feel." And that is most true within the parameters of theology. In the sciences, that is inconsequential. The causal factors always equal the same result. And that is hard and fast. But in the teaching work I do, that is not how it works. The heart and the brain are on equal footing.

How do you make sure your teaching is based on correct principles?

The short answer is that you have to have an understanding of what is the baseline, the foundation upon which everything else rests. For me, that is the example and the person, Jesus Christ. That is my foundation. If a teaching passes the litmus test—that it is a pleasing teaching to Jesus—then I am good with that.

Let me be really clear. I don't always get that right. I am not suggesting that I have figured out the code. But that is my baseline. I always ask, "What is the heart of Jesus in this matter?" And I answer that by investigating the Gospel narratives—Matthew, Mark, Luke, and John—as well as other scripture passages. And then I try to find parallels in my own life. Those are the stories I have to tell. And I try to tell them.

Several virtues are evident in this pastor's story about how he improves instruction.

Understanding:
Coming back I can tell you that teaching in the church is always about getting to know the people well enough to know the questions they are asking. Then, if you are trying to influence them in the long run, you need to give them something they can hold in their hand. So, hard copies of the things I would be teaching back then were essential.
Eventually, I realized I was trying to keep up with technology, but people were not asking technological questions. They wanted to know things of the heart and how the heart and mind work together to produce meaningful faith.
I have discovered that my lack of technological knowledge has never become a factor for most of the congregants. They are looking for a personal connection. They are not looking for me to replicate what they experience in their technological world.

Imagination:
Maya Angelou reminds us that, "It is not a matter of what someone tells us or tries to teach us, it is how they make us feel." And that is most true within the parameters of theology. In the sciences, that is inconsequential . . . But in the teaching work I do, that is not how it works. The heart and the brain are on equal footing.

Strong Character:
It was a good stretching experience. I am so grateful for it. With the college students changing every year, I had to learn what college students in general were asking in addition to what a particular college student was asking. Where are they going? What is at the core of who they are?

Humility:
The good news for me is that I now serve a church that has four associate pastors—a pastor of students, a pastor of families, a pastor of creative

worship, and an associate pastor. They are all wonderful, and they are also technologically savvy.

I always ask, "What is the heart of Jesus in this matter?" And I answer that by investigating the Gospel narratives—Matthew, Mark, Luke, and John—as well as other scripture passages. And then I try to find parallels in my own life.

INSTRUCTOR 9 (GOODWILL TRAINER)

Background

Instructor 9 is responsible for training new Goodwill employees. They call it "GPS onboarding."

Day 1 of the training is when I educate participants on the history of the organization, our vision, our mission, our values and standards of behavior. I answer the question, "What do we expect from you as an employee?" Day 1 is interpersonal and about the employee. Day 2 is devoted to the paperwork we need from them, and the HR staff takes care of that.

In response to the pandemic, my first task was to take our entire onboarding program and convert it into an e-learning module. I worked with our HR generalists to make sure all the HR information was up to date. I also had to do an entire lesson on how CDC guidelines need to be enforced in our retail stores.

Creating this module took about one month. It was created to be presented to all new employees at all levels of the organization—the stores, the career centers, and the executive staff. We try to set our new hires up for success. If our regional Goodwill office hires you, you have to complete the two-day onboarding training.

With a bachelor's degree in communications, I was able to quickly pick up some of the things they wanted me to do. Since completing the e-learning module for onboarding, I have developed over ten other e-learning modules. I developed job descriptions for our retail division—to make sure employees know what is expected of them when they have a certain job title. I also worked closely with our safety coordinator to develop safety modules.

I've developed fifteen modules since the onboarding transition in March. I finally have time to reflect. My graduate school semester ended. I am pursuing an MBA.

With this reflection time I was able to review all my modules and edit my portfolio. There is a world of difference between the modules I created in March and what I am creating now. Now I am going back and tweaking things to be more aesthetically pleasing and effective.

How has your instruction evolved over your first two and one-half years?

When I was hired in June 2018, I was sent to Atlanta to complete a three-day workshop on effective training and facilitation, sponsored by the Association for Talent Development (ATD). I also became a member of that association. From them I receive notifications about webinars and different workshops. I have taken several webinars through ATD and Development Dimensions International (DDI).

Once I completed that workshop, I was thrown into the hustle and bustle of traveling to facilitate onboard training. I took what I learned in that workshop and it was trial and error from there.

I remember the first time I facilitated onboarding. I had a huge facilitator's guide that I held close to me because I was not yet familiar with the material. As I facilitated the same material from week to week, I grew more confident. I was able to share clarifying anecdotes. In the beginning I wanted to make sure I said everything that was highlighted in the notebook. After six months in the role, I never touched the notebook because by then I knew the material.

As far as dealing with my participants goes, I worked in retail for many years, so I had learned about dealing with different personalities. Retail helped me become a people-person and know how to deal with different personality types.

Whenever Day 1 of onboarding would begin, and the HR generalist would hand out the paperwork, that was my opportunity to scan the room. I made it look like as if I was not paying attention to the class, but I was listening to those side conversations. I was hearing everything.

Then, when I finally would speak, I let everyone know:

> "You are going to be my troublemaker, today, so I will watch out for you."
> "You are falling asleep, so you better go back and get some coffee right now. I need you awake for five or six hours, minimum."

We have three onboarding training sites. We have varying ages and education levels of participants. During the icebreakers, when they introduce themselves, I learn that some of them are recent high school graduates and this is their first job; some are senior citizens who want to get out of their homes and find meaningful work; some are Project Re-entry (recently released from prison) participants and they are starting their lives over. We train all different types of people from different backgrounds.

We also have professional/career-level participants. I facilitated onboarding with a vice president as a participant once. That makes the dynamic different each time. As the instructor, I have to meet everyone where they are.

If the person is a vice president of an organization, I can use huge words all day long, and they can keep up. But for someone who cannot fill out their paperwork or properly type on a laptop, I have to help them understand the message I am trying to get across.

When I am scanning the room, I am listening for all sorts of things. Sometimes, when the HR generalist is moving around the room doing different things, participants roam to the snack/coffee area, and they chat among themselves. It is nervous energy. It is part of norming and forming a group.

So, I start to hear conversations. "Man, I almost overslept this morning." Or, "I just got off from my other job. I came straight here, and I am super tired." Those are the things that guide me as I facilitate our day together.

In the beginning of my tenure, I was strongly encouraged to stretch the onboarding sessions from 8 am to at least 4 pm. But I don't like to waste people's time. If I can get all the messages across in less time, and we are finished at 2 pm, that is fine. Most people don't want to be in there any longer, anyway. And I gauge that. You have the chatter boxes who can sit and talk all day. And then you have the people who are distracted because they have to get their kids or take care of other duties.

It is a lot to juggle. I ask myself, "How am I going to make this day work for everyone—so everyone is comfortable, and I can get my mission accomplished."

I decide on how to make that happen when I analyze what happens after the icebreaker. When they are finished with the icebreaker and they are sitting with their team and they've given themselves a name and talked about what they have in common, then I see the different personalities. I notice the introverts, and I know I am not going to get much out of them. I recognize that others are ready to talk with me all day. On the other hand, I have had people tell me, "I am just ready to get this over with."

We do evaluations after each onboarding session. When I first began in this role, I read every evaluation because I wanted feedback. I wanted people to be honest and tell me what they liked and what they did not like. The most recurring theme was, "It's very long. I enjoyed it, but it is very long."

I heard that, so I thought, maybe I can get away with shaving off an hour or two. Eventually I was able to do that and it was not a problem. I think the turning point for me was, after the first six months, my confidence in knowing the material grew and my confidence in myself grew.

This is my first facilitator role. I did a lot of public speaking in my youth—via church and my grandmother putting me in talent shows. So, getting in front of a crowd wasn't scary. It was the realization that "Oh my gosh. There is so much material to learn."

When I shadowed my predecessor before she left the organization, I wondered, "How does she remember all of these dates, acronyms, and programs?" It was overwhelming.

How do you make sure your instruction is based on correct principles?

The big turning point for me was the fall of 2019, when I took an organizational behavior course in my MBA program. I already knew about Maslow's hierarchy of needs, but I also learned about Herzberg and motivation theory and hygiene factors. And I learned about different types of leadership. I learned about transformational leaders, Theory X and Theory Y, and how different types of managers and leaders behave.

Fall of 2019 was the light bulb for me. I thought, this is one course that is applicable to everything I do on a regular basis in my role as a trainer. Organizational behavior is all about learning how people behave in a workplace setting. It is important to understand what you can expect from managers, to understand the difference between decisions that are made from the top-down or bottom-up. All of that is important.

Motivation and hygiene factors are very important to me because, once you realize what people are truly there for, you know how you can meet their needs. The participants who are tired because they just got off another job are very low on the hierarchy of needs. All they care about is survival. All they care about is, "I need to make sure my bills are paid." They might not even be on the second level yet, where they have achieved safety and security.

On the other hand, a person who was a vice president in a previous role and earned a decent salary is comfortable. That person thinks, "This is a new opportunity for me. This is intriguing. I can sit and chat with you all day." Realizing what people need, what motivates them, and what is going to get the reaction and participation that I need is important.

This is a learning environment. I have to remind myself of that whenever I step into the classroom. Yes, it is new hire orientation, but they are in session for two days. I need to figure out what types of personalities are in front of me as quickly as possible. Then I can navigate the way this course goes for the day. That is important for a facilitator—to be able to pinpoint the personalities.

To me that is the most important. You can know the material like the back of your hand, but the most important challenge is knowing how to deal with people, how to recognize personalities, especially the difficult ones, the know-it-alls, the cynics, and the attention seekers. You have to be able to recognize them very early in the day. If you don't, the probability that you lose control of the room throughout the day rises astronomically.

What do you do to make your instruction clear and simple?

When I first began facilitating, I read the guide, which is very wordy. When I began, I probably sounded like a robot reciting those paragraphs. With my public speaking background, I realized I couldn't just read to them. So, I highlighted all the important points. I realized I needed to put my spin on it. I have to use the verbiage that works for me. I am still going to tell them the facts, the figures, the information they need. I won't manipulate that, but I will manipulate the words I choose to get that out. I had to eliminate the extra fluff. I know what they need to walk away with, and I make sure I cover that and reiterate it.

We also have a participant's guide for both days. As we work through the presentation, there are blanks they fill in. Sometimes, after I have spoken about something, I ask them if they caught the answer to a particular blank. Or I will say, "We are going to go over page two before you go on your break." That allows me to see who is hearing me. If a lot of participants are struggling to recall the information I just provided them, then I make sure I repeat it. Repetition is important. Sometimes you have to repeat it three times in order for participants to process the information.

Aside from the MBA course in organizational behavior last fall, I've completed several webinars since March. Before then I wasn't able to attend workshops because I was on the road every day or every other day. There was no time for me to sit down and develop my skill set further. With the pandemic, since March, I have been able to personally develop my instructional design skill set.

One of my colleagues studies neurology, and she enjoys sending out articles about those kinds of topics and how they are applicable to learning & development. And I like having those conversations when we get together. I like change. That is why I love this industry. I realize everyone learns differently. E-learning and instructional design are forever changing because technology is forever changing. We have to be agile and keep up with it so we can meet the learners where they are.

Several virtues are evident in this Goodwill trainer's story about how she improves instruction.

Understanding:
During the icebreakers, when they introduce themselves, I learn that some of them are recent high school graduates and this is their first job; some are senior citizens who want to get out of their homes and find meaningful work; some are Project Re-entry (recently released from prison) participants and they are starting their lives over. We train all different types of people from different backgrounds.

We do evaluations after each onboarding session. When I first began in this role, I read every evaluation because I wanted feedback. I wanted people to be honest and tell me what they liked and what they did not like. The most recurring theme was, "It's very long. I enjoyed it, but it is very long."
The big turning point for me was the fall of 2019, when I took an organizational behavior course in my MBA program.
Fall of 2019 was the light bulb for me. I thought, this is one course that is applicable to everything I do on a regular basis in my role as an HR Trainer. Organizational behavior is all about learning how people behave in a workplace setting.

Imagination:

Whenever Day 1 of onboarding would begin, and the HR generalist would hand out the paperwork, that was my opportunity to scan the room. I made it look like as if I was not paying attention to the class, but I was listening to those side conversations. I was hearing everything.

Strong Character and Generosity:

I realize everyone learns differently. E-learning and instructional design is forever changing because technology is forever changing. We have to be agile and keep up with it so we can meet the learners where they are.

Courage:

In the beginning of my tenure, I was strongly encouraged to stretch the onboarding sessions from 8 am to at least 4 pm. But I don't like to waste people's time. If I can get all the messages across in less time, and we are finished at 2 pm, that is fine. Most people don't want to be in there any longer, anyway. And I gauge that.

INSTRUCTOR 10 (HR CONSULTANT, SPECIALIZING IN TEAM BUILDING)

How has your instruction evolved?

I remember watching the movie, *Patch Adams*. It was about valuing the quality of one's life. I had my entire life and career figured out. I was going to be a doctor; I was going to be Patch Adams. And the reason I was so compelled by this movie is that he was able to impact people by genuinely connecting with them, even though he was not the smartest or best clinician.

Having said that, I took a chemistry class and realized that ten years of medical school was not going to work out, which shifted me into instruction. That was a huge piece of my evolution because I am much more interested in the way people learn. What I have seen in the Hollywood version (*Patch Adams*) and in the actual classroom is that people learn better, they are more curious, and they are more engaged when they are connected with the instructor and with each other.

If the instructor has no interest in being there, like my calculus professor in college, little is going to be learned. She said she didn't want to be there, so I dropped that class fast. I didn't get to lesson two.

Sometimes people stay in classes, even though they have checked out. Their bodies are present, and one half of their brain is present, but that is not learning to me. That is like learning stuff to forget it quickly.

The second big evolution is that in college I had the most memorable instructor of my life. I took an abnormal psychology class, and each class covered a different psychological disorder—phobias, schizophrenia, or eating disorders. In each class you would do something experiential and visual. For example, for phobias, he brought in a six-foot rat snake. He talked about how all of us are on a continuum of phobias: As he walked closer to the student, he said, "You might not be scared of the snake when it is here, but how about when it is here?" That was twelve years ago, and I remember many different experiences in that class. But, for lots of teachers, I would say that I don't remember any specific class. So, I recognized that the visual and experiential aspects of a class can make it meaningful.

Third, I learned about overcoming resistance to learning. One of my early jobs was to sit in a group of six to twelve college students and facilitate a dialogue about race relations, other conflicts, politics, and religion—soft fluffy topics (sarcasm). And the students were forced to be there for class credit. So, everybody came in with their arms crossed. They did not want to sit in a circle and talk about race with a bunch of strangers for 90 minutes.

The data we collected on those students later indicated that 98% of them started leaning in. Many said they would voluntarily come back for a second conversation. That was a big learning moment for me. I learned that if you can get students to meaningfully connect with each other's personal stories, about things they care about, learning will occur. Most instructors say, "Get into break-out groups and talk about physics." That is fine, but there is something different that happens in a person's brain when they talk about what is important to them. That has influenced a lot of the way I do instruction.

How do you make better connections with your learners?

I ask a lot of questions. As I craft a workshop or a YouTube video, I never do it in my own cave. I involve people in the process. In all the videos I address questions people have asked me in some capacity.

Soon I will be sending an email to those on my company list of followers. It will say, "Hey, I am going to be on Zoom at this time. For any of you who have been watching videos, I want to know what you love, what is frustrating, what I could do to improve them." So, I am asking for their feedback to continuously improve the way I instruct.

I have learned to let go. I might be attached to some things that I do, but if they annoy students, I should just stop doing them or reconfigure them in some way. So, I am asking for feedback on their learning.

How do you make your instruction clear and simple?

One thing I have bought into is a technique called "pink sheets," created by a guy out of Australia. It starts with an 8.5 by 11 inch piece of paper. He would say that if you fill out that piece of paper, it is a full spectrum idea, as opposed to when we have just one little part of an idea. If we have a story, that is one part of an idea. If we have a metaphor, that is one part of an idea. If we have data, that is one part of an idea. If we have a quotable saying, that is one part of an idea. And if we have a diagram, that is one part of an idea. A "pink sheet" is one main idea with a metaphor, data, a story, and all the stuff explaining it. I have created hundreds of pink sheets for the topics I instruct on.

So, when I instruct in a YouTube video, I might say, "Intentions influence impact, but they don't control it." Behind that for me is a personal story, a metaphor, and the other things. That pre-thinking allows me to do much more improvised teaching with less preparation. And one of the reasons I do that is because I am a terrible procrastinator.

If I have a workshop with 300 faculty at a university tomorrow at noon, I won't start prepping until 9 am. That is not totally true because I have created hundreds of these pink sheets. I have mapped out all of these ideas beforehand. So, when I am asked a question, I have thought about it to some degree. But the actual flow does not get written on my iPad or in my notebook until the day before or that morning.

The pink sheet procedure allows me to create simplicity. It is actually annoyingly complex and they are not in any particular order. When I look at a pink sheet, I often think, "I am not sure how I will present this to a group."

That is why I still need to do an outline. For me, that is a more linear process: here is the order of activities and the things I am going to say and the framings. And I know the ingredients I need to inject in order for this course or class to be interesting. There needs to be an unofficial start. There needs to be a hook. There needs to be connection before content. There needs to be visual or experiential content. And there needs to be a really deliberate closing. Those are easy to put together because I have done the more complex things first. So, complexity happens behind the scenes. Simplicity happens in front of the scenes.

Using the pink sheets allows me to easily create those five ingredients. Having that framework allows me to see where I have the blanks to fill in on my outline.

How do you make sure your lessons are based on correct principles?

If I am teaching something, I need to have tried it many times beforehand. Or I tell people that the technique or activity we are doing is an experiment. The other thing is that going back to the pink sheets, in order to fill in the data category on every one of the hundreds of pink sheets are a ton of primary resource articles, a ton of books, a ton of people who are smarter than me living in that corner of the pink sheet, bringing out their educational experiences.

For example, on one of my pink sheets, there is a description of a meta-analysis study that says knowledge of students' and instructor's personal backgrounds creates communication shortcuts and improves learning outcomes. So, if I break students into small groups and they do an exercise in which they report on something they have recently discovered and are excited about, I know that will eventually create communication shortcuts. So, I am doing activities that are based on my psychology background.

When I was offered admission to a PhD program in psychology, I realized that I am more interested in what actually works in the moment. After that I am interested in what is rooted in some sort of data. I lean more heavily on the practitioner end of things. Does this work in the classroom on Tuesday at noon when I try it? If it does or doesn't, then I decide if I should do it.

The practitioner aspect is like comedians refining their skits. They go to smaller clubs to test out their jokes. In teaching, if I talk to a group and ask them, what are the five ingredients for engaging learning, and they can't recount any of them, then I have to change the way I share them.

Several virtues are evident in this story about how a consultant improves his team-building instruction.

Understanding:
That was a big learning moment for me. I learned that if you can get students to meaningfully connect with each other's personal stories, about things they care about, learning will occur . . . there is something different that happens in a person's brain when they talk about what is important to them. That has influenced a lot of the way I do instruction.

Soon I will be sending an email to those on my company list of followers. It will say, "Hey, I am going to be on Zoom at this time. For any of you who have been watching videos, I want to know what you love, what is frustrating, what I could do to improve them. So, I am asking for their feedback to continuously improve the way I instruct.

Imagination:
I ask a lot of questions. As I craft a workshop or a YouTube video, I never do it in my own cave. I involve people in the process.

A "pink sheet" is one main idea with a metaphor, data, a story, and all the stuff explaining it. I have created hundreds of pink sheets for the topics I instruct on.

And I know the ingredients I need to inject in order for this course or class to be interesting. There needs to be an unofficial start. There needs to be a hook. There needs to be connection before content. There needs to be visual or experiential content. And there needs to be a really deliberate closing. Those are easy to put together because I have done the more complex things first. So, complexity happens behind the scenes. Simplicity happens in front of the scenes.

So, if I break students into small groups and they do an exercise in which they report on something they have recently discovered and are excited about, I know that will eventually create communication shortcuts.

Strong Character and Generosity:
In teaching, if I talk to a group and ask them, what are the five ingredients for engaging learning, and they can't recount any of them, then I have to change up the way I share them.

Conclusion

Several instructors said they consider research findings, but, in the end, they used whatever worked in their situation. And, toward the end of her story, Elementary School Teacher 3 said, "There was a lot of trial and error that year."

That sentence describes how teachers improve instruction within the aesthetic paradigm. Within the social science improvement paradigm, however, trial and error are less desirable than "best practices" or evidence-based practices. That is why professors of education conduct studies and publish findings that are evaluated for statistical significance, validity, and reliability. If that were not the purpose of educational research studies, professors of education would tell aspiring teachers to use trial and error to determine what works for their students. But that would be too simple. Professors like to make things complicated.

In other words, if we shifted to an aesthetic improvement paradigm—because teaching is an art—professors of education would teach aspiring teachers to use their understanding of the situation to come up with imaginative ways to improve learning. They would also explain that teachers need to bring the character virtues (strength and courage) and the spiritual virtues (humility and generosity) to the situation. Many of the twenty-seven stories describe that process.

One other interviewee comment is noteworthy before completing this discussion of the difference between the two paradigms. It comes from the physical therapist, who is the only interviewee trained in the medical model for improving treatments—the model that is mimicked in the social science improvement paradigm.

Instructor 2 said,

Just because we learned something a certain way does not mean there isn't new research out there that disproves it. I try to remember that, just because I was tested this way and this is how we learned it, that may not be true anymore.

You really have to separate personal anecdotes and personal experience from the research. You also have to look at research with discernment and understand its goals and parameters. You can find an article to back up anything you want it to. You can also find articles to negate something.

An example of K-12 teachers believing in debunked research is that several of the interviewees said they vary their methods to match student learning styles. Psychologist Daniel Willingham has been debunking the learning styles theory for more than twelve years (https://video.search.yahoo.com/yhs/search?fr=yhs-mnet-001&hsimp=yhs-001&hspart=mnet&p=daniel+willingham+learning+styles#id=1&vid=28ff88b01ada22cf00177186cd3fcc96&action=click). Although it seems to make sense to believe that students have different learning styles, research on this topic has failed to find evidence that learning styles exist. But nothing is lost if teachers believe in this idea. It means their imaginations are activated as they create different kinds of activities for students.

For the past seventy years the improvement paradigm situation in education has been similar to medieval times, when Catholic astrologers tried to explain the movement of heavenly bodies, based on a geocentric paradigm—the earth is the center of the universe. Their efforts were futile, until Copernicus and Galileo changed the paradigm to a heliocentric one—the sun is the center of our solar system. Similarly, it is essential to adopt the correct paradigm for improving education. To do this we should ask teachers how they improve. A productive line of questioning is to ask which virtues they bring to the learning situation.

Bibliography

Brookfield, S. D. (2006). *The Skillful Teacher.* 2nd Ed. San Francisco: Jossey-Bass.
Gardner, H. (2000). *The Disciplined Mind.* New York: Penguin Putnam.
Hurley, J. C. (2009). *The Six Virtues of the Educated Person.* Lanham: Rowman and Littlefield Education.
Jalongo, M. R. and Isenberg, J. P. (1995). *Teachers' Stories: From Personal Narrative to Professional Insight.* San Francisco: Jossey-Bass.
Kelly, J. L. (Winter, 2019–20). *Learning Connections*, p. 21.
Palmer, P. (1994). Leading from within: Out of the shadow into the light. In J. Conger (Ed.), *Spirit at Work* (pp. 19–40). San Francisco: Jossey-Bass.
Peck, M. S. (1978). *The Road Less Traveled: A New Psychology of Love, Traditional Values, and Spiritual Growth.* New York: Simon & Schuster.
Sarason, Seymour A. (1999). *Teaching as a performing art.* New York: Teachers College Press.
Schubert, W. H. and Ayers, W. C. (eds.) (1992). *Teacher Lore: Learning from Our Own Experience.* New York: Longman.
Sternberg, R. (1996). *Successful Intelligence: How Practical and Creative Intelligence Determine Success in Life.* New York: Simon & Schuster.

About the Author

J. Casey Hurley taught and coached at Xavier High School in Appleton, Wisconsin, from 1974 to 1977. He earned a master's degree in educational administration from the University of Wisconsin-Madison in 1978. He was an intern assistant principal at Columbus High School in 1978–1979, and he was the development director at Edgewood High School, Madison, Wisconsin, from 1979 to 1982. He was an assistant principal at Stoughton High School from 1982 to 1985, before becoming principal of Lodi High School in 1985. He earned a PhD in educational administration from University of Wisconsin-Madison in 1989 and was a professor of educational administration at Western Carolina University (WCU) until retirement in 2019. He is the author of *The Six Virtues of the Educated Person* (2009) and is currently professor emeritus at WCU.

www.ingramcontent.com/pod-product-compliance
Lightning Source LLC
Chambersburg PA
CBHW020750230426
43665CB00009B/558